Sudden Infant Death Syndrome

Peggy J. Parks

LUCENT BOOKS

A part of Gale, Cengage Learning

GALE
CENGAGE Learning

Detroit • New York • San Francisco • New Haven, Conn • Waterville, Maine • London

LIBRARY OF CONGRESS CATALOGING-IN-PUBLICATION DATA

Parks, Peggy J., 1951–
  Sudden infant death syndrome / by Peggy J. Parks.
    p. cm. — (Diseases & disorders)
  Includes bibliographical references and index.
  ISBN 978-1-4205-0202-2 (hardcover)
  1. Sudden infant death syndrome—Juvenile literature. I. Title.
  RJ320.S93P37 2009
  618.92'026—dc22

                                                    2008047168

Lucent Books
27500 Drake Rd.
Farmington Hills, MI 48331

ISBN-13: 978-1-4205-0202-2
ISBN-10: 1-4205-0202-6

Printed in the United States of America
1 2 3 4 5 6 7 13 12 11 10 09

Table of Contents

Foreword   4

Introduction
    "In One Moment My Life Shattered"   6

Chapter One
    What Is SIDS?   10

Chapter Two
    What Causes SIDS?   26

Chapter Three
    The SIDS Diagnosis   40

Chapter Four
    Surviving the Aftermath of SIDS   56

Chapter Five
    SIDS in the Future   70

Notes   85

Glossary   91

Organizations to Contact   92

For Further Reading   96

Index   99

Picture Credits   103

About the Author   104

"The Most Difficult Puzzles Ever Devised"

Charles Best, one of the pioneers in the search for a cure for diabetes, once explained what it is about medical research that intrigued him so. "It's not just the gratification of knowing one is helping people," he confided, "although that probably is a more heroic and selfless motivation. Those feelings may enter in, but truly, what I find best is the feeling of going toe to toe with nature, of trying to solve the most difficult puzzles ever devised. The answers are there somewhere, those keys that will solve the puzzle and make the patient well. But how will those keys be found?"

Since the dawn of civilization, nothing has so puzzled people—and often frightened them, as well—as the onset of illness in a body or mind that had seemed healthy before. A seizure, the inability of a heart to pump, the sudden deterioration of muscle tone in a small child—being unable to reverse such conditions or even to understand why they occur was unspeakably frustrating to healers. Even before there were names for such conditions, even before they were understood at all, each was a reminder of how complex the human body was, and how vulnerable.

While our grappling with understanding diseases has been frustrating at times, it has also provided some of humankind's most heroic accomplishments. Alexander Fleming's accidental discovery in 1928 of a mold that could be turned into penicillin has resulted in the saving of untold millions of lives. The isolation of the enzyme insulin has reversed what was once a death sentence for anyone with diabetes. There have been great strides in combating conditions for which there is not yet a cure, too. Medicines can help AIDS patients live longer, diagnostic tools such as mammography and ultrasounds can help doctors find tumors while they are treatable, and laser surgery techniques have made the most intricate, minute operations routine.

This "toe-to-toe" competition with diseases and disorders is even more remarkable when seen in a historical continuum. An astonishing amount of progress has been made in a very short time. Just two hundred years ago, the existence of germs as a cause of some diseases was unknown. In fact, it was less than 150 years ago that a British surgeon named Joseph Lister had difficulty persuading his fellow doctors that washing their hands before delivering a baby might increase the chances of a healthy delivery (especially if they had just attended to a diseased patient)!

Each book in Lucent's Diseases and Disorders series explores a disease or disorder and the knowledge that has been accumulated (or discarded) by doctors through the years. Each book also examines the tools used for pinpointing a diagnosis, as well as the various means that are used to treat or cure a disease. Finally, new ideas are presented—techniques or medicines that may be on the horizon.

Frustration and disappointment are still part of medicine, for not every disease or condition can be cured or prevented. But the limitations of knowledge are being pushed outward constantly; the "most difficult puzzles ever devised" are finding challengers every day.

"In One Moment My Life Shattered"

On September 2, 2003, Cathy Meinecke gave birth to her fourth child, a baby boy she and her husband named Brenden. He was born prematurely, but was healthy and normal. The day the Meineckes were able to take their new son home from the hospital was joyous for them. Their family was now complete, and they considered their lives perfect. Then, in the early morning of October 9, the unthinkable happened. The Meineckes found eighteen-week-old Brenden dead in his crib. They had put him to bed the night before, and he went to sleep and never woke up. The baby died of a disorder known as sudden infant death syndrome, or SIDS. "They say life can change in an instant, but it seems unbelievable until it happens to you," she writes. "In one moment my life shattered. . . . I lost my son and my life in one horrific moment."[1]

A Cruel and Secretive Killer

The Meineckes' tragic story is just one of thousands. SIDS, which is sometimes called crib death, claims the lives of more than two thousand babies each year in the United States. It is the leading cause of death among infants aged one to twelve months and the third leading cause of overall infant mortality. Yet SIDS remains mysterious to scientists. Seemingly healthy, happy babies who are developing normally suddenly die without warning, usually in their sleep. Bob Cringely's son, Chase,

SIDS is a mysterious disorder in which seemingly healthy babies die suddenly, usually in their sleep.

died of SIDS in April 2002 at the age of two and a half months. Cringely describes what happened: "He literally stopped breathing lying in my lap while I did e-mail. There was no sound, no struggle. I just looked down and he was no longer alive. I have no idea whether he had been dead for one minute or 10, but we were unable to revive him. He was never sick, he just died, and now there is a void in our lives that we can never fill."[2] Because no cause of death is obvious when babies die of SIDS, it remains baffling to scientists and health-care professionals. Since it cannot be prevented, many parents of young babies live in fear of it.

Sometimes when parents hear the diagnosis of SIDS, they feel relief knowing that their baby's death could not have been prevented. Henry Krous, a pathologist from San Diego, says that SIDS is a very comforting diagnosis for grieving parents because it assures them that they were not responsible for their child's death. Other parents, however, are not consoled to hear that their babies died of SIDS. "They simply do not know why my daughter died," says April Poole, whose baby girl died from SIDS in 2005 at the age of ten weeks. "I put her to bed and she never woke up. In my opinion, whether it's called 'unknown' or SIDS is one [and] the same to me."[3] Whether learning that SIDS was responsible for a child's death is comforting or not, anyone who loses a child—especially for no apparent reason—is devastated. This was the case with Aaron and Rachal Tallent who live near Phoenix, Arizona. On the evening of June 10, 2007, they went for a long walk with their four children. Eleven-year-old Joey accompanied the family on his skateboard. Morgan, age six, rode in a stroller along with his two-year-old sister, Arielle. Baby Jaiden, who was three and a half weeks old, slept soundly in the stroller basket. About two hours later the Tallents returned home. They fed Jaiden, played with him for a while, and dressed him in animal print pajamas. Then they kissed him, told him they loved him, and tucked him into bed for the night.

Aaron left for work early the next morning. Rachal prepared a bottle and went into the bedroom to feed Jaiden. He was not moving or making any sounds, so she thought he was asleep—

but when she picked him up, she saw that he was not breathing. After a panicked call to 911, paramedics arrived and rushed the baby to the hospital, while the Tallents followed. When they reached the hospital, a crushing blow awaited them: The doctors had not been able to revive Jaiden. Aaron and Rachal were consumed with grief, as she explains:

> He was so cold . . . all I wanted to do was warm him. . . . I couldn't put him down, I wanted to take him home, I needed him to be ok. . . . We couldn't let it sink in that he was really gone, our baby that completed our family, the love of all our lives. . . . No words can describe how a mother's arms ache after losing her baby, no one can understand how bad your heart can ache for a baby that is no longer around.[4]

The Tallents learned that their baby had likely died of SIDS.

Shrouded in Mystery

Unlike other infant disorders, SIDS is not something that can be detected ahead of time or prevented. It is a frightening, mysterious disorder that can strike any infant, anywhere, at any time, without warning. Babies who appear perfectly healthy and happy one day just fall asleep and die. Their parents are left feeling sick at heart, often wondering if they could have done something to save their child. Because so much remains unknown about this tragic killer of babies, scientists aggressively continue to study SIDS. It is their goal to gain a better understanding of why it claims the lives of so many infants each year. Hopefully, they will solve the mystery someday. Until then, however, thousands of babies remain at risk.

CHAPTER ONE

What Is SIDS?

Most life-threatening diseases or disorders that strike infants can be clearly defined. Leukemia, for example, is a known cancer of the blood. Meningitis is an inflammation of the fluid in the spinal cord and around the brain. Hepatitis is an infection of the liver. Pneumonia is an inflammation of the lungs and respiratory system. Throughout the years, scientists have studied these and other diseases and have gained significant knowledge about them. But sudden infant death syndrome is nothing like other childhood diseases. When a baby dies suddenly and un-expectedly, and no reason can be found, the death is often attributed to SIDS. According to a March 2004 *FBI* [Federal Bureau of Investigation] *Law Enforcement Bulletin*, SIDS claims more infant lives in the United States each year than genetic defects, illnesses, injuries, and homicides combined.

"Remorse and Horror"

Although the SIDS diagnosis is relatively new, the sudden, un-expected death of infants has been recorded throughout history. References to babies dying of unexplained circumstances appear in the Bible, as well as in other historical books and literature. In the first century B.C., the Greek historian Diodorus Siculus wrote about Egyptian mothers whose babies had died

Memorial statue in a cemetery dedicated to babies who died in infancy.

Studies have shown a connection between SIDS and babies who sleep on their stomachs.

unexpectedly. The women were accused of "overlaying" (smothering) the infants as they slept together in the same bed. Rather than being executed, as was the typical punishment for murder or negligence, the women were condemned to hold the dead babies in their arms for three days and nights. D.L. Russell-Jones explains that this was intended to make the mother "experience her full deserts of remorse and horror."[5]

It was not until the mid-twentieth century that scientists began to examine unexplainable infant deaths to see if they shared any common traits. Harold Abramson, a physician from New York City, analyzed infant deaths for four years during the 1940s. He found that 68 percent had been sleeping on their stomachs, and nearly half were found with their noses and mouths against bedding. In 1944 Abramson published a paper in the journal *Pediatrics*, in which he stated that the babies had died of accidental suffocation. Many disagreed with his theory and were angered by it. In the early 1950s pathologists Jacob Werne and Irene Garrow published a paper that denounced what Abramson had written. They claimed that mothers whose babies had died were already suffering from indescribable guilt and grief, and blaming infant deaths on suffocation just increased those feelings. Instead, wrote Werne and Garrow, there had to be medical issues involved in the deaths, most likely related to infections.

The first conference on the cause of sudden infant death was held in Seattle, Washington, in 1963. Afterward, the written proceedings pointed out the urgency of studying those deaths in greater detail:

> One is startled to find that the number of infants who die of the sudden death syndrome is of a comparable order of magnitude to the number of adults who die from carcinoma [cancer] of the lung. Despite this fact the information is miniscule in comparison to that on carcinoma of the lung. The many questions raised by this conference should provide a stimulus for more comprehensive and detailed studies from this and other countries.[6]

An Official Diagnosis

A second conference on causes of sudden infant death was held in 1969. A lead presenter was J. Bruce Beckwith, a physician from Seattle. Beckwith's objective was to show evidence that most infants who died unexpectedly share some similarities, and he speculated that common threads connected them. Participants engaged in a number of heated discussions but eventually agreed with Beckwith. In order to focus attention and research on the problem, as well as provide a certifiable cause of death, he urged his colleagues to adopt a diagnosis. His suggestion was "sudden infant death syndrome," because the word "syndrome" implied a combination of causes. The group approved and officially defined SIDS as: "the sudden death of any infant or young child, which is unexpected by history, and in which a thorough post-mortem examination fails to demonstrate an adequate cause for death."[7]

Although Beckwith was relieved that SIDS was finally an official diagnosis, he was very unhappy with how it was described.

He explains: "If a prize were offered for the poorest definition of a disease or disorder in the scientific literature, this one would be a strong contender!"[8] He thought the description was far too general and should include the various similarities shared by SIDS victims. For example, virtually all the babies studied had been found dead after being put down to sleep. Age was another common factor, as most infants were between two and four months old. Also, far more infant deaths occurred during the winter months than in warmer seasons. In spite of Beckwith's arguments, however, the original SIDS definition remained unchanged for twenty years. It was not until 1989 that the wording was revised to specify infants less than one year of age.

In 1990 the National Institute of Child Health and Human Development expanded the SIDS description, wording it as follows: "The sudden death of an infant under one year of age which remains unexplained after a thorough case investigation, including performance of a complete autopsy, examination of the death scene, and review of the clinical history."[9] This was more comprehensive than the 1989 definition, which did not call for an examination of the death scene.

The Highest Risk

In the years since SIDS was given a name and a description, scientists have learned more about it. In the process, they have become much more aware of its risk factors. By far, the most prominent risk is the infant's age. An estimated 95 percent of all SIDS cases strike babies who are between one and six months old. Angi Suby, a young mother from Minnesota, lost her three-month-old son, Stephen Paul, to SIDS in July 2007. She had taken him to the doctor for what she thought might be an ear infection, but he said the baby just had a cold. Suby returned home, and as she was taking Stephen out of his car seat, he opened his eyes and flashed a big smile at her. Then he closed his eyes again and went back to sleep. She put him in his bed for a nap—and when she checked on him twenty minutes later, she was horrified to find him dead. Suby was shocked because she and her husband had done everything

Being Prepared

When SIDS strikes, babies abruptly stop breathing. Because of that, many parents install breathing monitors, which register an infant's breathing and/or movement. When the monitor detects a substantial gap in breathing, it sounds an alarm. These devices have reportedly helped to avert tragedy by alerting parents that their infants had breathing problems. Still, however, the issue of breathing monitors is controversial. The American Academy of Pediatrics says no evidence has been found that breathing monitors can prevent infants from dying of SIDS. One concern is that they provide parents with a false sense of security. If parents rely solely on the monitor's alarm, they may not check on their baby as often as they should. In that case, if a monitor did not function properly and failed to detect a gap in breathing, the child could die. Another

concern is that monitors send out false alarms, which can cause parents or caregivers to disregard one that might actually be signaling a problem.

There is controversy over whether the use of a baby monitor is helpful in preventing SIDS.

Premature babies born to mothers younger than twenty years old are at greater risk for SIDS.

possible to prevent SIDS, and yet their baby had still died. "In just a matter of 20 minutes he was gone," she writes. "I still see his blue mouth and how limp he was when I held him. . . . He has been our angel right from the beginning. Now he's our angel with wings. I miss him so much it hurts."[10]

After the age of six months, an infant's risk of dying from SIDS markedly declines. In rare cases, however, SIDS does claim the lives of older babies. Cooper Joshua Eason was two months shy of his second birthday when his father found him dead in his crib. Cooper had been a healthy, happy toddler who was loving and easygoing, a joy to his family. His favorite movie was *The Wizard of Oz*, which he often watched on DVD while singing along with "Somewhere over the Rainbow." His unexpected death was devastating for his parents and his three-year-old sister Olivia. His mother describes it as "the most gut wrenching, heartbreaking, nauseating, ridiculous time of my life. My boy, my beautiful perfect healthy 22-month-old baby boy was dead."[11] Yet as tragic as Cooper's death was, for a child over the age of one to die of SIDS is extremely rare. As Beckwith had observed and noted at the SIDS conferences, the largest number of victims are between two and four months old.

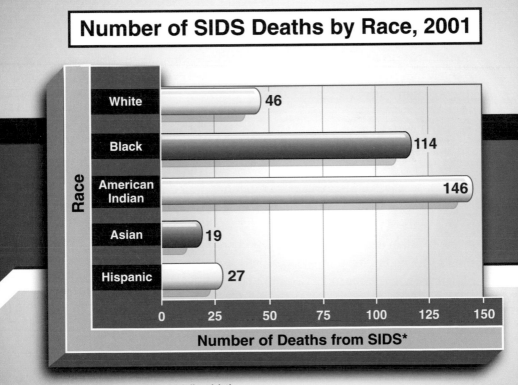

Number of SIDS Deaths by Race, 2001

White 46
Black 114
American Indian 146
Asian 19
Hispanic 27

Race

Number of Deaths from SIDS*

*Rate per 100,000 live births

Taken from: National Sudden and Unexpected Infant/Child Death & Pregnancy Loss Resource Center. www.sidscenter.org/SIDSdeaths.html.

SIDS is also more likely to strike babies who are born prematurely, have low birth weight, or whose mothers received no or poor prenatal care while pregnant. Another high-risk group is mothers who are younger than twenty years old. The American SIDS Institute offers this advice: "Don't get pregnant during the teenage years. If you are a teen and already have one infant, take extreme caution not to become pregnant again. The SIDS rate decreases for babies born to older mothers. It is highest for babies born to teenage mothers. The more babies a teen mother has, the greater at risk they are."[12] SIDS victims share other similarities as well. Boys, for example, are at greater risk of dying from SIDS than girls. An estimated 60 percent of SIDS cases are male infants, while 40 percent are females. Race is also a factor. African American infants are two times more likely to die of SIDS than Caucasian infants. The SIDS cases among Native Alaskan and Native American infants are three times higher than among white infants and two times higher than in the United States as a whole. Scientists say the reason that male and minority infants have a higher risk of being stricken with SIDS is not clearly defined.

How Prevalent Is SIDS?

Although babies continue to die of SIDS, the Centers for Disease Control and Prevention (CDC) reports that the number of SIDS-related deaths has decreased significantly since the 1980s. According to the CDC, from 1980 through 1988, 47,932 infants born to residents of the United States died from SIDS. That was an average of 5,326 deaths per year. In 1992 an estimated 4,895 babies died of SIDS. By 2004, the last year for which data are available, SIDS cases had reportedly dropped to 2,247.

Not everyone agrees that those statistics are correct, however. Even though SIDS deaths appear to have declined, the *overall* number of infant deaths has remained relatively steady since the 1990s. Thus, a number of health-care officials and researchers question whether a decline in SIDS deaths has occurred at all. The CDC's John Kattwinkel explains: "A lot of us are concerned that the rate (of SIDS) isn't decreasing significantly. . . . It is still a very high killer of babies."[13] A report published in October 2007

Unusual SIDS Stopper

The American Academy of Pediatrics recommends that babies less than one year old be given a pacifier for bedtime and naps. The reason? Pacifiers have been shown to help reduce the risk of SIDS. Physicians at the University of Virginia announced in April 2006 that when infants sleep with a pacifier in their mouths, their risk of developing SIDS drops by 61 percent. In a separate study by Kaiser Permanente and the National Institutes of Health, researchers also found that a pacifier helps to prevent SIDS. This is true even if the babies were exposed to risk factors such as stomach sleeping or secondhand smoke. Scientists are not sure why a pacifier lowers SIDS risk. Possibly it helps a baby wake up more easily, and/or perhaps the pacifier positions the tongue in such a way that the airway is kept open.

The American Academy of Pediatrics recommends that babies sleep with a pacifier to reduce the risk of SIDS.

by Scripps Howard News Service reinforces Kattwinkel's point of view. It details the results of a seven-month investigation of forty thousand infant deaths tracing back to 1992. One finding is that many health officials and medical examiners would not classify infant deaths as SIDS. Even though SIDS is widely accepted as the cause of unexpected infant deaths, some physicians do not believe in the concept of SIDS. Their contention is that SIDS is an invalid diagnosis. So, they write vague terms such as "undetermined cause" or "sudden and unexplained death" on death certificates. Another finding is that twenty-two states rely on coroners to diagnose death rather than medical examiners. Coroners, who are generally not required to be doctors or even have medical training, were 37 percent more likely than medical examiners to use a diagnosis of "undetermined cause" on infants' death certificates.

Angie Steffke is a woman from Indianapolis whose eight-month-old son died unexpectedly in 2003. After the autopsy report stated "undetermined causes," the grieving mother was left feeling empty and confused. She explains: "It is a horrible, horrible thing to be told that no one knows why my baby died." A police detective informed Steffke that the state of Indiana no longer used the term SIDS to define unexpected infant deaths. "That really upset me because they want to say that SIDS is happening less often," she says. "But there are no fewer babies dying. They are just calling it 'undetermined causes.'"[14] Kattwinkel and others who share Steffke's viewpoint fear that the actual number of SIDS cases could be significantly higher than what is being reported.

Life-Threatening Events

Whether SIDS cases are actually declining remains an issue of controversy. Nevertheless, scientists continue to aggressively pursue research to learn more about SIDS in an effort to prevent infant deaths. They are also studying what is known as apparent life-threatening event syndrome, or ALTE. Occurring mainly in babies who are less than one year old, ALTEs do not usually result in death. Instead, they are considered close calls, and are characterized by a frightening collection of symptoms.

For no apparent reason, a healthy, active baby just abruptly stops breathing (known as apnea), or begins to choke or gag. The skin of babies stricken with ALTE changes color, becoming pale, bluish, or blotchy. Their bodies often become stiff and then limp, and they appear to be near death. Some sort of resuscitation is typically required in order to revive a baby who has suffered from an ALTE.

Prior to the 1980s pediatricians often referred to such episodes as "near-miss SIDS." They believed that the baby would likely have died of SIDS if he or she had not been discovered in time. This was never proved, however, and in 1986

A mother shows how CPR is performed when a baby needs to be resuscitated.

the National Institutes of Health Consensus Panel concluded that ALTE could not definitely be linked with SIDS. Thus, the name was changed to apparent life-threatening event syndrome to distinguish the episodes from SIDS and to more accurately reflect what was happening to babies.

Kimberly de Montbrun will never forget the night her three-month-old son suffered a life-threatening event. She had nursed him to sleep, and then she lay down beside him so that she could sleep herself. A few hours later she was suddenly jolted awake by fear. She knew that something was very wrong, as she explains:

> My mind was screaming "LOOK AT THE BABY!" I looked over to where he lay beside me, but he was too still. The room was dark, but he glowed a ghostly white in it. My heart pounding out of my chest and a pain in the pit of my stomach, I lay my hand on his chest, reassuring myself that sometimes the eyes play tricks and that he was fine. I leaned my face close to feel the heat of his breath . . . but it was not there.[15]

Fear and dread washed over De Montbrun, and she felt as though she were living in a nightmare. She placed her hand on the baby's chest and rubbed it, but he still did not move or breathe. Then she began rubbing his chest again,

> but this time more urgently, the way that you would rub a newborn pup or kitten to get them to breathe. Suddenly he took a ghastly breath in. So deep and sudden, it filled the entire room with its gasp and lurched his tiny chest in the air. It sounded like he was sucking the life back into him, and he was. After that he breathed normally. I held him on my chest, with his ear to my heart to remind him to keep going, and cried. In the morning I took him to our pediatrician, but was anything but consoled. Sometimes these things just happen. Sometimes babies have apnea. Sometimes they resume breathing on their own. Sometimes they don't.[16]

After that, De Montbrun lived in fear every time she put her baby to bed, and she wondered if she would ever again be able to sleep normally. She writes:

What if it happened again? My mommy senses had woken me up the first time, but could I count on them again? How could I live with myself if something happened (something . . . I can't even bring my mind to even think the words) and I didn't wake up? The fear was overpowering. It tainted every moment. . . . [M]y baby almost died and I felt helpless.[17]

The baby never had another episode, but De Montbrun still lived in fear every day. She said it was such a terrifying experience that she probably would always be haunted by it.

Even though no direct connection has ever been found, babies have died of SIDS after they suffered from an ALTE episode. According to physicians Karen Hall and Barry Zalman, studies have shown that between 4 and 10 percent of babies die of SIDS after experiencing a life-threatening event. This is especially true of babies who suffered from other disorders, such as seizures or irregular heartbeat. Hall and Zalman add that babies who experience ALTEs have a greater likelihood of sudden death than those who have not.

"The Hardest Thing I Have Ever Had to Do"

Although scientists know more about SIDS today than they did in the past, it is still baffling to them. They know that most babies who die of SIDS are between two and four months old, although younger and older babies are also at risk. A dramatic drop in SIDS cases seems to have occurred since the 1980s, but even that is in question. Are fewer babies actually dying today of SIDS, or are their deaths just being labeled with other names? No one can say for sure. Another controversial issue is whether apparent life-threatening events are in some way connected to SIDS. Many health officials see no connection; others are not so sure. The only certainty is that SIDS deaths are devastating to those who are left behind. One person who knows that firsthand is Jessica Jackson, whose thirteen-week-old son died of SIDS on December 12, 2007. She describes the agony of that day in the hospital:

Mothers who have lost a baby to SIDS describe the experience as an intense and painful grieving process.

They escorted me behind the curtains where my little boy laid there motionless on a gurney wrapped in a blanket. I picked him up and held him and cried and cried and cried. I held him for two hours. I kissed him and sang to him and was looking at him and just hoping that he was sleeping. He was so heavy and so cold. I sat there and held him for two hours until he started turning blue. I then realized I couldn't look at him like this. . . . I kissed him 3 times symbolizing the phrase, "I LOVE YOU." I hugged him and then did it again. I turned around and walked away. That was the hardest thing I have ever had to do in my life was to walk away from my child . . . forever.[18]

CHAPTER TWO

What Causes SIDS?

Jessica and Ed Tamblin are boating enthusiasts who always look forward to the summer months. For years they have docked their cabin cruiser on a lake in Wisconsin, where they spend every weekend from late spring to early fall. After their twin boys were born, the four of them often stayed on the boat. They spent their days enjoying the sun and water, and at night they slept together at night in a large bed. Everything about their lives seemed to be going well, and they were very happy—until June 2000 when tragedy struck. The Tamblins woke up in the morning and found one of the twins, Justin, unusually still and silent. His skin was cold to the touch, and when they picked him up, he was unresponsive. They called 911 and tried to resuscitate him, but they could not. At the age of seven months, Justin was dead. His parents were devastated, feeling as though their happy life had suddenly been shattered.

Although years have passed since Justin's tragic death, Jessica Tamblin says that horrible day is permanently etched in her mind. She still cannot help crying whenever she talks about it. "It is impossible to describe the gut-wrenching pain Ed and I went through," she says. "There are just no words. We wondered, how could this happen? Why did our baby die? Could we have done something to save him?"[19] When the cause of death was ruled to be SIDS, the Tamblins had mixed feelings, as Jessica explains:

> In one way we were relieved to know it wasn't our fault, that there was no way we could have kept him from dying. But it really didn't do much to comfort us because the fact is, SIDS is a "nothing" diagnosis. It means nothing. Absolutely nothing. If they can't find anything that went wrong, they chalk it up to SIDS. For parents who desperately want answers, hearing something like that can leave you feeling pretty hollow inside.[20]

Perspectives on Bed Sharing

The Tamblins' grief over losing their baby was worsened by all the publicity that followed his death. Since the cause of the baby's death was not immediately known, newspaper articles speculated that Justin could have suffocated while sleeping in the same bed as his parents. "It was just not true," says Jessica,

> and it killed us to read that. The bed was huge and there was plenty of room for the babies and us. Neither of us rolled over on Justin—he was on the other side of the bed! And there weren't blankets on his face or anything like that. He just went to sleep and died. That's what happens with SIDS babies—they just die and no one knows why. Sometimes I wonder if newspaper writers even know how much damage their stupid assumptions do to people, and how cruel they are when they write things they know nothing about. It just hurts us so bad to think about it even now.[21]

Whether adults should sleep in the same bed with their babies is a controversial issue. Many health organizations, including the National Institute of Child Health and Human Development, urge parents never to sleep with infants. The Mayo Clinic says that adult beds are not safe for babies because they can become trapped and suffocate between headboard slats, the space between the mattress and bed frame, or between the mattress and the wall. The American Academy of Pediatrics (AAP) agrees,

Victorian-Era Theories

Today, it is well known that SIDS and suffocation are two completely different causes of death. This was not the belief years ago, however. During the mid-1800s infants who died suddenly were assumed to have been smothered by their mothers. Brendon Curgenven presented a paper titled "The Waste of Infant Life," which stated:

> Suffocation at the mother's breast is the most common form; this frequently occurs on Saturday night; the mother, it may be, has been drinking, or goes to bed late; takes her child to her breast; falls asleep, and awakes in the morning to find her infant dead. In most cases the child's head slips off the mother's arm during sleep, its face becomes buried beneath the breast, the bed-clothes at the same time covering its head; it dies without a struggle suffocated by the carbonic acid exhaled from its own lungs. In winter these cases of suffocation occur most frequently in consequence of the mother unconsciously drawing the bed-clothes over her own shoulders.

Quoted in D.L. Russell-Jones, "Sudden Infant Death in History and Literature," *Archives of Disease in Childhood*, 1985, p. 279.

saying that bed sharing is more hazardous to babies than sleeping in their own cribs. A study published in the medical journal *Pediatrics* in November 2006 also linked bed sharing to several SIDS risk factors. The study focused on 239 babies from New Jersey who died of SIDS between 1996 and 2000. The researchers were from the SIDS Center of New Jersey at the University of Medicine and Dentistry of New Jersey–Robert Wood Johnson Medical School. In looking for patterns among bed-sharing babies who died of SIDS, the team found that 39 percent of them died while sharing a bed or couch. Those babies were more likely to have sleep risks such as sleeping with soft, loose bedding (pillows, quilts, or blankets) or to have slept in the same bed as other children.

Many people, including a number of physicians, do not believe that bed sharing puts babies at higher risk for dying of SIDS. Chiropractor Linda Folden Palmer, who authored the book *Baby Matters*, strongly disagrees with the AAP and other organizations that warn against bed sharing. She explains:

> Reviewing study after study, the message is clear: The relative risk of death for infants sleeping in a safe adult bed with a safe parent is not greater than those found sleeping next to the parental bed, and their death risk is far smaller than those sleeping in a crib in another room. And, for infants over 2 or 3 months of age, the studies show a protective effect of co-sleeping over sleeping next to the parental bed.[22]

Authorities disagree on whether parents sharing a bed with their baby puts the baby at greater risk for SIDS.

Palmer says that the AAP's recommendations against bed sharing are based on "sensationalized incomplete findings."[23] She cites one study that was done with 200 California infants who had died of SIDS. The researchers found that 45 of the infants died while co-sleeping: 35 were sharing their parents' bed, 6 were sharing a babysitter's bed, and 4 died while sleeping in their mothers' arms. Thus, co-sleeping was found to occur in only 22.5 percent of the SIDS deaths. At the end of the study, the authors reported "no significant relationship between routine bed sharing and the sudden infant death syndrome."[24]

A major source of controversy over parents sleeping with infants is the theory that bed sharing reduces the risk of SIDS. According to professor of anthropology James J. McKenna, several studies have proven this to be true. One that was done in Saskatchewan, Canada, showed that SIDS cases were reduced among babies who co-slept with their mothers and were breast-fed. A study in South Africa showed that co-sleeping babies had

Deadly Mattresses?

Researchers throughout the world are studying SIDS in an effort to find the cause. One controversial theory is that SIDS is caused by toxic gases inside crib mattresses. In order to make mattresses flame retardant, chemicals such as phosphorus and arsenic are added during manufacturing. A fungus that commonly grows in bedding reportedly interacts with the chemicals to create poisonous gases. These heavier-than-air gases are concentrated in a thin layer on the baby's mattress or are diffused away and dissipated into the surrounding atmosphere. If a baby breathes or absorbs a lethal dose of the gases, the central nervous system shuts down, stopping breathing and then heart function. These gases can fatally poison a baby without waking him or her and without any struggle by the infant. A normal autopsy would not reveal any sign that the baby was poisoned.

higher survival rates than infants who slept alone. In Hong Kong, where co-sleeping is a normal family practice, SIDS rates are among the lowest in the world. This is also true in other Asian countries, as McKenna explains: "SIDS and infant mortality rates in general are decreasing to record low levels in Japan in parallel with increases in nighttime 'bedsharing.' In most other Asian cultures where cosleeping is also the norm (China, Vietnam, Cambodia and Thailand) SIDS is virtually unheard of."[25]

De Montbrun is convinced that co-sleeping saved her baby boy's life. He was in bed with her the night that he suddenly stopped breathing. Because she instinctively knew that something was wrong, she woke up and was able to revive him. "I do not mean to imply that co-sleeping can prevent all SIDS deaths," she writes:

> It is a mysterious killer, and the answers are still to be found as to why so many babies are silently stolen from their parents. . . . What I do know is that I sensed something that night. A change in the little body that lay next to me. And that change woke me up. Would that have happened if he had been in a crib away or a room away from me? Could I have sensed a difference that far? I don't know the answer but I cannot bring myself to think of what [might have] happened if my son had not been in my bed that night . . . if I had chosen to follow the advice of countless people and parenting "experts" and had him in his own crib. It sends a chill down my spine.[26]

"Back to Sleep"

Although bed sharing is a widely debated issue, most scientists and health-care professionals agree on some risk factors for SIDS. One is that infants should always be placed on their backs to sleep. Studies have repeatedly shown that far more infants die from SIDS while sleeping on their stomachs. Betty McEntire, director of the American SIDS Institute, explains: "[M]ore convincing than any other fact is that belly-sleep has up to 12.9 times the risk of death as back-sleep."[27] Exactly why back sleeping reduces the risk of SIDS is not known, but scientists

The presence of stuffed animals in a crib introduces the risk that they will block the airway of a sleeping baby.

do have theories about it. One is that stomach sleeping puts pressure on the infant's jawbone, which causes the airway in the back of the mouth to become narrower and hampers the ability to breathe. Another common theory is that stomach sleeping increases a baby's risk of rebreathing his or her own exhaled air. This is especially true when babies sleep on very soft surfaces or are surrounded by blankets, stuffed toys, or pillows. Exhaled air contains carbon dioxide, which is toxic when inhaled. When babies breathe it, the oxygen level in their bodies drops, and carbon dioxide accumulates in the lungs.

The concept of stomach sleeping versus back sleeping was originally born in Australia, New Zealand, and England. Health officials in those countries discovered that a much lower incidence of SIDS occurred when babies were placed on their backs to sleep. After hearing of these findings, the AAP endorsed the back sleeping concept. In 1992 the organization officially recommended that babies sleep on their backs for their first year of life. As a follow-up to the AAP's recommendation, in 1994 the National Institute of Child Health and Human Development launched a far-reaching publicity campaign known as Back to Sleep. At that time an estimated 70 percent of infants in the United States were sleeping on their stomachs. By 2002 the number was believed to have dropped to just over 11 percent. Many people credit the Back to Sleep program with the steady decline in SIDS deaths, as the AAP explains: "Since 1992, and consistent with a steady decrease in the [stomach] sleeping rate, there has been a consistent decrease in the SIDS rate."[28]

Back sleeping cannot necessarily prevent SIDS, however. When Angi Suby put her baby Stephen Paul in bed for his nap, she placed him on his back. She made sure that he was not too warm or too bundled up. She also made sure that no stuffed toys or pillows were anywhere near him. Still, in spite of these precautions, SIDS claimed the baby's life. The same is true of many other babies. They still die of SIDS even though the parents do everything possible to reduce the risk, including placing them on their backs to sleep. That is one reason why some people reject the idea that a connection between SIDS and stomach sleeping exists. Increasing numbers of parents are placing their babies on their stomachs because they sleep more soundly that way. They believe that the benefits of sound sleeping outweigh the rare risk of SIDS. In an informal poll, which involved more than twenty-four thousand users of the Web site BabyCenter.com, nearly half of the respondents said that their babies slept on their stomachs. Those who advocate stomach sleeping say that doctors tell parents what they should do without living in the real world. Erica Lyon, who is a newborn-care instructor and the director of the RealBirth center in New York City, explains: "I'm very sympathetic to the mother who is so sleep-deprived that she puts the baby on its belly knowing that all the experts recommend not to. The role of the professional is to say 'these are the recommendations and this is why.' The role of the parent is to think critically and apply those recommendations in a way that makes their life manageable."[29]

The Smoking Connection

Even though people disagree over the role back sleeping plays in the development of SIDS, scientists say that smoking is a definite risk factor. Studies have shown that infants of mothers who smoked during pregnancy have a higher risk of dying of SIDS—as much as three times higher than babies whose mothers did not smoke. Exposure to secondhand smoke has also been linked to SIDS deaths. Health officials say that exposure to secondhand smoke doubles a baby's risk of SIDS death. According to William H. Gershen, an associate professor of pediatrics at the Medical College of Wisconsin, many SIDS deaths could be prevented if babies were not exposed to smoke either in the womb or after they have been born. He explains: "Believe it or not, probably the biggest risk factor for SIDS identified by current research is smoking, especially smoking by the mother. . . . Both smoking while the baby is in the womb and second-hand smoke after birth appear to be risk factors."[30] Studies suggest that smoking may affect the central nervous system of babies while they are still in the womb. If they continue to breathe secondhand smoke after they are born, they have a higher risk of developing SIDS than babies who are not exposed to smoke.

A study that was published in *Sleep Review* magazine in March 2008 reinforced the connection between smoking and SIDS risk. The study, which was conducted with laboratory rats, was based on the knowledge that when babies are in the womb, they receive oxygen from the mother. When they are born, they are exposed to lower oxygen, which signals their

Smoking during pregnancy and around babies has proven to be a risk factor for SIDS.

glands to release chemicals that cause them to instinctively take their first breath and make their heart beat more efficiently. This protective mechanism remains in place for the first few months of the baby's life. After that, the central nervous system takes control and the mechanism is no longer needed. But according to the study, when babies are exposed to cigarette smoke (especially while they are still in the womb) the mechanism does not function long enough. Thus, the babies have a much higher risk of developing SIDS than infants who are not exposed to smoke.

"Was It the Vaccines?"

Scientists generally agree about certain risk factors for SIDS, such as smoking. But another possible risk factor—childhood vaccinations—is much more controversial. Health officials from the CDC and other organizations say that no evidence of a causal relationship between SIDS and vaccines has been found. But many parents, as well as some doctors and researchers, are convinced that a link exists. This belief is based partly on the fact that numerous vaccines are routinely given before a baby is six months old, which is also the period of time when SIDS is most prevalent. According to the National Vaccine Information Center, a Food and Drug Administration database contains nearly five hundred reports of children who died of SIDS during the 1990s within three days of receiving the diphtheria, tetanus, and pertussis (DTP) vaccine. Of those reports, 58 percent listed SIDS as a "reaction" to the shot.

A 1985 study in Australia revealed startling findings regarding the connection between vaccinations and SIDS. Scientists Viera Scheibner and Leif Karlsson studied the breathing patterns of babies who had been immunized. They found that the infants' breathing was affected in a certain characteristic manner for forty to sixty-five days after they had received DTP vaccines. They also interviewed a number of parents who had lost babies to SIDS and learned that most of the babies had died after DTP injections. They concluded that an undeniable link between SIDS and vaccinations exists. Scheibner went on to study thousands of medical papers that dealt with vaccinations.

A doctor gives a baby a vaccination. Some doctors and parents believe there is a link between infant vaccinations and SIDS.

She was shocked to discover that no evidence existed in the papers about the effectiveness and safety of vaccines. "Cot (crib) death is caused by vaccines," says Scheibner. "Vaccines are noxious substances. Serum of SIDS babies are so poisonous that all mice injected [with] minute amounts of it die."[31]

Shelly Walker, who lives in Idaho, is convinced that vaccines can lead to SIDS. Walker's four-month-old son Vance was a happy, healthy baby whom she describes as "extremely full of life, energy and vitality."[32] In September 2007 Walker took him to a pediatrician's office for his vaccines. In one fifteen-minute visit, the baby was given a dose of Pediarix, which is a five-in-one shot for diphtheria, tetanus, pertussis, hepatitis B, and polio, as well as several other vaccines. Less than three days later Walker woke up at 5:15 A.M. and realized that the baby was unusually quiet. "I went to pick him up and then I screamed,"[33] she says. Vance was still warm but he was not moving. Blood had crusted beneath his eyes, and bloody foam coming from his mouth was on his clothes and bedding. She frantically tried to resuscitate him while her husband called 911. But when the family arrived at the hospital, emergency room doctors told them that Vance was dead. They were consumed with shock and grief, as Walker explains: "I grabbed my baby in my arms and held him up and I screamed, 'How . . . did this happen? Was it the vaccines?'"[34] Vance's death was ruled to be SIDS, but Walker has no doubt that the vaccinations were responsible. She became even more certain when she learned about two other recent SIDS deaths. One baby died a week before Vance, and the other died a month later—after both of them had received the same vaccines at the same pediatrician's office.

Will the Cause Be Found?

Whether vaccinations contribute to the development of SIDS is not known with any certainty. But because such a link is possible, scientists continue to investigate the connection. They are also pursuing many other studies in an effort to find what causes SIDS. Although much progress has been made, scientists are the first to admit that all they have are theories. Smoking is thought to be a high risk factor, and many health-care professionals believe that stomach sleeping is as well. Issues such as co-sleeping and vaccinations are highly controversial, with strong viewpoints on both sides. Because SIDS continues to kill several thousand babies each year, and because there is no proven way that it can be prevented, researchers and health-care officials feel a sense of urgency to find what causes it. According to Kattwinkel, SIDS is as mysterious today as it always has been. "If we knew exactly what causes it," he says, "we wouldn't call it SIDS."[35]

CHAPTER THREE

The SIDS Diagnosis

One of the most tragic aspects of sudden infant death syndrome is that by the time it is diagnosed, the baby has already died. There is no way to diagnose it when a baby is still alive. Equally tragic is that SIDS cannot be prevented. Even parents who take all the recommended precautions to reduce risk may still lose babies to SIDS. When it is finally diagnosed, it is because all other possible causes of death have been ruled out, as the AAP explains: "A diagnosis of SIDS reflects the clear admission by medical professionals that an infant's death remains completely unexplained."[36] Actually, a diagnosis of SIDS is not a diagnosis at all, but rather the *absence* of one. Because of that, it is often called a diagnosis of exclusion.

The SUID Investigation

Before SIDS is diagnosed, an investigation usually takes place. One essential component is a thorough examination of the death scene by law enforcement officials. Although these visits and the questions that are asked can be painful for grieving parents, this step is crucial in order to diagnose the death correctly. Investigators initially call the death a sudden, unexplained infant death (SUID). The Federal Bureau of Investigation (FBI) recommends that a SUID be treated like any other mysterious death.

Unlike illnesses that have symptoms, such as a fever, SIDS cannot be diagnosed until it is too late.

FBI agent Ernst H. Weyand explains: "A meticulous investigation must begin immediately to determine if criminal behavior caused or contributed to the death of a child. . . . [W]ithout a complete investigation, the circumstances surrounding a baby's death will remain a mystery."[37]

Weyand says that officers should be dispatched immediately to the hospital or other location where the baby was pronounced dead, as well as visit the location where the baby was first discovered. At the hospital, investigators examine the body and take photographs. At the location where the infant was found, officers often collect physical evidence such as the baby's clothing, bedding, formula, prescription or over-the-counter drugs or medications, and any toys that were located near the baby. The officers interview family members or other caregivers and then document their findings. They record observations about the general cleanliness of the home, the number of people living there, and what the baby's sleeping surface was like. They ask questions such as whether an adult was sleeping with the baby at the time of death, and if the person was impaired by drugs or alcohol. Another important aspect of the investigation is a review of the infant's medical history. Officers gather information about the baby's last doctor's visit, immunizations and when they were given, and whether the baby has ever been hospitalized or received emergency room attention. The family's case history is also carefully reviewed. For instance, investigators need to know about any suspicious childhood accidents or child abuse and whether other unexpected infant deaths have occurred in the same family. They also ask whether anyone in the house smokes, how the home is heated and ventilated, and what went on in the house during the hours before the baby was found.

The autopsy, performed by pathologists or other skilled medical professionals, is also essential in order to properly diagnose why an infant died. They lay the baby on a table for an external examination, noting factors such as the color and condition of the eyes, fingernails, arms, legs, and head. They also make notations about the color of the skin and whether marks, bruises, or signs of abuse or trauma are evident. They take

A Nevada coroner in an autopsy room. In 2006 the Centers for Disease Control and Prevention issued a protocol for investigating sudden unexplained infant deaths (SUID).

blood and fluid samples to check for any harmful substances that could have contributed toward the death. According to the AAP, this is a crucial part of the autopsy because it is the only way to know if a baby was poisoned, either deliberately or accidentally. One review cited by the AAP showed that seventeen out of forty-three infants who unexpectedly died before two days of age were found to have cocaine in their bloodstream.

The internal exam begins once the external exam has been completed. Pathologists examine and photograph vital organs and tissues to look for possible medical problems that were not evident when the baby was alive. Start to finish, the autopsy can take three or four hours. But it can take a very long time before the results are compiled, a diagnosis is made, and parents receive the death certificate. In some areas, medical examiners do their best to keep parents informed and provide them with a preliminary autopsy report within a few days. This is not true everywhere, though. Some coroners will not offer

Infant Botulism

The only way SIDS can be diagnosed is by performing an autopsy—but in some cases, the autopsy is wrong. In the January 2005 issue of the *Journal of Clinical Microbiology*, researchers wrote about an eleven-week-old boy from Finland who died unexpectedly in January 2002. The baby had been healthy and was developing normally, and pathologists who did the autopsy said he had died of SIDS. But further investigation showed that they were not correct. The baby had actually died of infant botulism, which is caused by botulinum, the most poisonous natural substance that exists. Botulism often occurs when an infant has been fed natural honey, even when a small amount of honey is used to sweeten a pacifier. In this baby's case, however, the botulism was not caused by honey. The baby died because of botulinum spores found in common household dust.

any information about the possible cause of death until all tests are in and have been reviewed by pathologists. In some cases, coroners refuse to discuss the infant's death or autopsy findings with the parents at all. Meta Dupuis, whose six-month-old son died of SIDS in March 1997, waited in a coroner's office for eight hours, and he refused to see her. Seven months passed before she received her son's death certificate.

"Where Was the Compassion?"

Many coroners, police officers, and medical professionals are sensitive toward grieving parents who have suddenly lost a child. They have a job to do, and that job is important. But they also know the parents are human beings who have just suffered a terrible, unthinkable loss. As the AAP writes:

> Most sudden infant deaths occur at home. Parents are shocked, bewildered, and distressed. Parents who are innocent of blame in their child's death often feel responsible nonetheless and imagine ways in which they might have contributed to or prevented the tragedy. The appropriate professional response to any child death must be compassionate, empathic, supportive, and nonaccusatory. . . . It is important for those in contact with parents during this time to be supportive while at the same time conducting a thorough investigation.[38]

Unfortunately, compassion and support were not what Darlene Buth and her husband experienced after the SIDS death of their four-month-old son Peter James (PJ). On October 3, 1995, Buth received an emergency phone call at work telling her that she needed to go home immediately. When she arrived, she saw a police officer standing in front of her house. She asked what had happened but he would not answer her. He simply told her to go inside. Nothing could have prepared her for what happened next. She learned that her husband had left the baby on the couch for a brief time. When he returned to the room, PJ's skin was a bluish color and he was not breathing. His father had called 911, and an ambulance rushed the baby to the hospital. When the Buths arrived, nurses ushered them into a small room and told them the pediatrician would be in to speak with them. The doctor walked in and said that he had done everything he could, but their son had died. "I just wanted to scream out, this isn't fair!" Darlene writes. "You can't take my little boy away from me!"[39] She and her husband went into an examination room where PJ was lying in a little crib. Darlene sat in a rocking chair and a nurse placed the baby in her arms. "They told us to say our good-byes," she says, "and all I could think of is, How do you say goodbye to your baby?"[40]

The Buths did not realize it at the time, but that was only the beginning of their nightmare. They returned home, shocked and numb, and were greeted at the door by police officers and social service workers. Darlene and her husband were instructed to go into different rooms so they could be interviewed separately. She was asked questions such as "How does your husband treat the children?" and "What kind of temper does your husband have?" She was also asked, "Has he ever lost his temper? Is he violent? Do you feel safe with him? Do you feel that the children are safe?" Darlene could not believe that she was being

Unfortunately, some parents become the target of an investigation after their baby has died from SIDS rather than receiving compassion after their loss.

scrutinized in this way mere hours after her baby boy had died. "I just couldn't understand what they were trying to do," she writes. "Where was the compassion? The caring? Where were the kind words? Why were they treating us this way? What did we do?"[41]

The Buths learned that because they had taken out life insurance policies on their children, they were suspected of murdering PJ in order to collect insurance money. They were stunned at the idea that they could be accused of something so terrible. Later they received the baby's autopsy report, which ruled his death as SIDS. After finding out what they had gone through, PJ's pediatrician called the police station. He said that he knew the family well, that they had no history of child abuse, and no foul play whatsoever had been involved in the baby's death. He added that the police were compounding the Buths' grief by unjustly hounding them. Darlene describes how she and her husband suffered through the investigation: "To be accused of killing our own child is something that I will never forget or understand. We loved our baby dearly and would do anything to bring him back. . . . Why do these people treat parents with so much contempt? If all their questioning is part of their job, why can't they figure out a better way of doing it? SIDS is a very tragic, painful experience, so why do they add to the pain?"[42]

When It Really Is Murder

What happened to the Buths was unfortunate because they were not found responsible for their son's death. But sometimes investigators learn that parents are to blame for the death of a baby, through either negligence or deliberate acts. The AAP states that although it happens in less than 5 percent of all infant deaths, fatal child abuse has been mistaken for SIDS. According to a study by Scripps Howard News Service, states that aggressively investigate infant deaths are finding twice as many homicides (known as infanticides) as states that do a cursory job of investigating the deaths. The study found that Arizona leads the country in detecting infant homicides, while Idaho has no formal review process for the deaths of children.

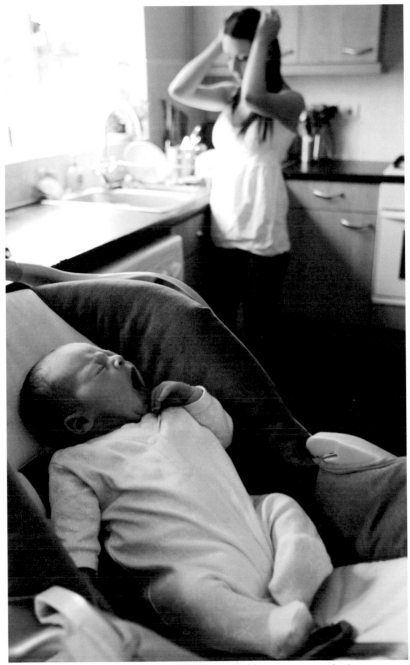

On rare occasions, mothers or fathers unable to cope with the strain of caring for an infant have killed their babies in such a way as to make it look like SIDS.

When Parents Kill

Law enforcement professionals often say that infanticide is difficult to detect. It is virtually impossible, for instance, for pathologists to tell the difference between babies who have been
smothered and babies who have died of SIDS. One particularly
disturbing fact is that some babies die because a parent, usually
a mother, has a disorder known as Munchausen syndrome by
proxy (MSP). A parent with MSP fabricates symptoms in his or her
baby, thus subjecting the child to unnecessary medical tests
and/or surgical procedures. Typically, an MSP parent takes the
baby to a medical facility and makes up a history of apparent
life-threatening events in order to deceive medical personnel.
Then, after the baby has been smothered or killed another way,
the MSP parent has a recorded history of being devoted and caring. Unless law enforcement officers have a specific reason to be
suspicious, the killer may unfortunately never be found out.

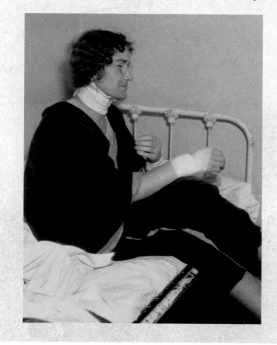

Police arrested
Harriet Paup in 1932
after she deliberately
cut her children and
herself on the neck
and wrists. Paup
suffered from
Munchausen
syndrome by proxy,
in which a parent,
usually the mother,
deliberately harms
his or her children.
Some health-care
professionals say that
staging such a crisis is
a bid by the parent
for attention.

As a result, the reporting of infanticides in Idaho is at least 14 percent below the national average.

One parent who committed infanticide was Kathleen Folbigg, a woman from Australia. On March 1, 1999, Folbigg reportedly found her nineteen-month-old daughter Laura in her bed, pale and cold with bluish-colored lips. She picked the baby up and rushed into the kitchen to call an ambulance. When the emergency team arrived, they found Folbigg sobbing as she performed cardiopulmonary resuscitation, or CPR, on her daughter. Laura was not breathing and paramedics could find no pulse. Later at the hospital, she was pronounced dead. During the autopsy the pathologist could find no apparent cause of death. But because of Laura's age, he believed she was too old to have died of SIDS. Instead, he ruled the death "undetermined" and ordered a police investigation. Detective Sergeant Bernard Ryan was assigned to the case. He began by interviewing Folbigg and her husband, Craig, and what he learned was shocking—Laura was the fourth of the Folbigg's children to have died unexpectedly. Their son Caleb had died at the age of twenty weeks. Another son, Patrick, had died when he was four months old. A daughter, Sarah, had died when she was eleven months old. In each of the cases, the children had been healthy and happy before they died, and their deaths were all ruled to be due to natural causes.

After Laura's death, Folbigg separated from her husband and moved out of their house. She left many possessions behind, including one of her diaries. One day as Craig Folbigg was doing some cleaning he found the diary and began to read it—and what he read, he later said, "made him want to vomit."[43] His wife had described in great detail her depression after each child's birth, and she said that she felt she was losing control. In one particularly revealing entry she wrote: "I feel like the worst mother on this earth. Scared that she [Laura] will leave me now. Like Sarah did. I knew I was short-tempered and cruel sometimes to her and she left. With a bit of help."[44] But the most chilling of all her writings detailed a terrible secret from her past. When she was eighteen months old, her father had stabbed her mother to death outside their home. On October 14, 1996, after three of her children had been found dead, Folbigg wrote the following: "Obviously I am my father's daughter."[45] Once Craig Folbigg realized what his wife had done, he turned the diary over to the police.

Ryan spent two years collecting evidence and assembling a case that he believed would result in Kathleen Folbigg's murder conviction. On April 19, 2001, police arrested her at her home, took her into custody, and charged her with four counts of murder. At her hearing, prosecutors claimed that she had deliberately smothered her children to death, and they produced the diary as the most incriminating evidence. They also presented a statement from forensic pathologist Janice Ophoven who said that the chances of all four children dying of SIDS "were a trillion to one."[46] Folbigg's trial lasted for seven weeks. On May 21, 2003, the jury of the Supreme Court of New South Wales found her guilty of killing her four children. The following August she was sentenced to forty years in prison.

SIDS or Suffocation?

Folbigg's case was highly unusual because whenever more than one infant death occurs in a family, police typically launch an investigation right away. Child abuse fatalities are very rare, though, and the cause of a sudden, unexpected infant death is often ruled to be SIDS because no official cause can be found. But in many cases, babies who actually die from suffocation are incorrectly diagnosed as dying from SIDS. Medical professionals often say that the two are very easily confused. "It is far more common for a child to die of asphyxiation than to die of SIDS," says Andrea Minyard, a medical examiner in Pensacola, Florida. "We say this with a heavy heart. But it is an accurate portrayal of what really is happening."[47]

A Scripps Howard study found that most coroners throughout the United States do not follow the CDC's standardized guidelines for death investigations. The guidelines call for an investigation of the death scene, performance of a complete autopsy, and review of the child's and family's medical history. There is, however, no federal legislation that mandates how infant deaths are investigated. Nearly all states have statutes re-

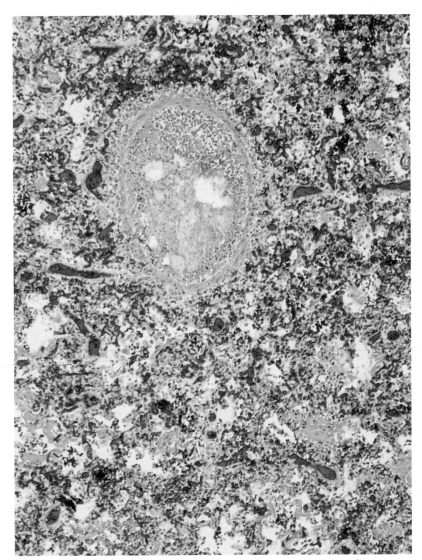

An airway of a SIDS victim. The similarities between SIDS and suffocation can cause medical professionals to confuse the two.

quiring that a death investigation occur in cases of sudden, un-expected death, but the actual performance of these investiga-tions varies widely from state to state, and even city to city. In some cases, the investigations may be done sloppily or may not take place at all. Thus, SIDS ends up as the diagnosis when the real cause of death is overlooked.

Another finding of the study is that eleven coroners who were adhering to federal guidelines when examining infant deaths in their communities found that 72 percent of the deaths were due to suffocation. In one Michigan county, nearly 90 percent of the fifty-eight babies whose deaths were investigated had been suffocated. On the opposite end of the spectrum, some communities reported low or no incidents of suffocation and had very high rates of deaths attributed to SIDS. In Omaha, Nebraska, for example, where sixty infants died unexpectedly over a five-year period, more than 90 percent were ruled to be SIDS deaths. Tom Haynes, Omaha's coroner, says it can be difficult to prove that a baby's death was caused by smothering rather than SIDS because grieving parents may withhold information. He explains: "We aren't doing this for humanitarian reasons. If the family doesn't admit to lying on top of the child during sleep . . . then we have no choice but to call it SIDS."[48]

A young mother named Kimberly Edge was convinced that her baby died from suffocation. On September 19, 2004, she went to check on Kaitlyn, her four-month-old daughter, who had been asleep for two hours. She had placed the baby faceup in the crib, but Kaitlyn had learned to roll over and was lying facedown when Edge found her. At first she thought the baby was still sleeping, but when she reached in to turn her over, she saw that her face and entire body were blue. Certain that Kaitlyn had suffocated, Edge began performing CPR and called 911. She could not revive her daughter, however, and at the hospital she was told that Kaitlyn did not make it. "I went running down the hall screaming and crying," she says. "It felt so unreal; I didn't know what to do. I wanted to hurt something, I ran outside the ER doors and leaned against the brick wall and started banging my head on it. I felt so much anger and pain."[49] Edge went back inside and was able to hold Kaitlyn for a couple of hours. A doctor came into the room and told her that her daughter had died of SIDS. She told him no, the baby had suffocated, which she believed because Kaitlyn was facedown and blue when her mother found her. The doctor assured Edge that Kaitlyn showed no signs of suffocation, and SIDS was ruled the official diagnosis. Yet for a long time she continued to question the diagnosis, and she posted a comment online in October 2007 about her uncertainty. "I have always wondered if she rolled over and because of her bedding being softer than the floor she couldn't roll herself completely," she wrote. "Could this be the case?"[50]

No Simple Answers

It is an undisputed fact that SIDS is a baby killer, but how often it is properly diagnosed is questionable. Some infant deaths that might have been attributed to SIDS have proved to be accidental suffocations, while in other cases babies were murdered. When comprehensive investigations take place after a baby dies, they result in the most accurate findings. But until these investigations are the norm for all infant deaths, uncertainty and inconsistencies are likely to figure in the diagnoses of sudden, unexplained infant deaths.

CHAPTER FOUR

Surviving the Aftermath of SIDS

People who have lost children to SIDS suffer from grief that seems unbearable. They wonder how they can go on living without their child, and they question whether they will ever be happy or normal again. They are overwhelmed by feelings of grief, guilt, and anger, and many become severely depressed. Melissa Eason experienced this sort of grief after her son Cooper died of SIDS in March 2006. She later wrote:

> It's only been 11 weeks since I was with my boy but it feels like 11 years. I don't want to do anything. I can't work, I can't stay home, I can't go back to OUR home, I can't stand, I can't sit, I can't eat, I can't sleep, I can't be alone but I can't be with people either. It's just impossible. Nothing else seems to matter to me. . . . My boy, my Cooper. I will never be the same person again. I will never be the "normal" happy person I once was. I will carry this around until the day I die and nothing will ever make it "OK." Cooper is etched into my heart, into my soul, into my body and mind forever.[51]

"Fear and Anger"

When parents, like the Easons, are the ones who find their child dead, it is horrifying for them. They must always live with that terrible memory, as Jessica Tamblin explains:

The grief from losing a child to SIDS is very hard for parents to bear.

To this day I still remember, in vivid detail, how cold and lifeless Justin was when we found him. At first everything was a blur, like this could not possibly be real. Then reality set in and I started screaming his name, willing him to wake up, but he was already gone, and I dropped to my knees and sobbed. Sometimes when I think about it even now my body starts to shake uncontrollably. You'd think I would be over it after all these years, but there is no way to get over something like that. Time does heal, I realize, but not completely. Never completely. The fact is, when your child dies, part of you dies too. I don't think either Ed or I will ever feel whole again. It's simply impossible to return to normal after a child has been ripped from your life.[52]

One fear that is commonly shared by people who have lost a child to SIDS is of having more babies. They are terrified that they will have to face losing yet another child. They also fear for the children they already have. Tamblin says that after her son died of SIDS she was consumed with fear that his twin brother would also be taken away from her. "I became fiercely protective of him," she says. "I watched him like a hawk and barely slept at night because I drove myself crazy jumping up to check on him, to make sure he was still alive and breathing. Ed did the same thing. For probably six months after Justin died we were like a couple of walking zombies."[53]

Cathy Meinecke was also afraid after her infant son Brenden died of SIDS, but her fear was mostly for herself. She wondered how she could possibly go on without him. She found that she could barely function, that she was just going through the motions of living. In the wake of her son's death she felt "lost, confused, hurt, angry, and scared." Meinecke says that she knew she had to survive, but she had no idea how she would do that. "Fear and anger is a constant companion after the death of a child," she writes. "Fear and anger crowd out so many of the more healing emotions, taking the space that love would normally occupy. I had to find a way to get beyond those emotions. . . . I was afraid if I did not keep moving forward I

Parents who have lost a child to SIDS sometimes find comfort in support groups composed of other grieving parents.

would stop and never start again."[54] She adds that her grief over losing Brenden radically changed her:

> I was a shell of the happy, bubbly woman I had once been. I could no longer believe that everything in life was going to be alright just because I was a good person. I had gone to church, prayed every day, volunteered for charity and cared about my fellow man. I had been a good wife, mother and daughter. I fit none of the criteria, in my mind, that warranted this punishment from the universe. And I had no idea of how to deal with this change in my paradigm.[55]

Meinecke tried to go back to living her life just as she had before Brenden died, but she found that to be impossible. Although she had never asked for any sort of help in the past, she realized that she could no longer face her grief alone. She needed to reach out to others and seek help, which she says was the most important step in her journey toward healing. She began going to conferences and camps for grieving families. She also sought out other bereaved parents because she knew that, unlike most other people, they personally understood what she was going through because they had experienced it themselves. "I could handle comments like, 'you're wallowing in pity,' because I respected the fact they had been there also," she says. "I could let them sympathize or be tough with me. At times, I became angry with them, only to realize my anger was not with those who were trying to help me. I was just angry—angry at the world. But, I could be less angry with someone who had also lost a child."[56]

Having a support network helped Meinecke cope with her grief, but she had still not found anything that could help her on an ongoing basis. So she turned to unusual therapies such as massage and aromatherapy. She also began to study Reiki, a Japanese technique for stress reduction and relaxation that also promotes healing. She says that Reiki helped her to start to restore balance in her life and health and to reconnect with her spirituality and faith. The combined therapies helped Meinecke relax and taught her about the importance of living in love rather than fear, as she explains:

Fear crowded my other emotions and left nothing for others, even in the best of times. I could not be complete when I was in such a negative space in my life. . . . As I healed my energy, I found that I was able to put fear and anger into perspective. . . . I found that what I had been longing for was right there when I knew how to reach for it. It had been there all along, even though so much of the time I had felt like it was lost.[57]

Meinecke believes that her life will always have a hole in it because of the loss of her son. But in the years since his death, she has become more and more able to heal and move forward. She is now a Reiki master who gives treatments to others and teaches them the techniques she has used for herself. "I take my life one day at a time," she says, "and try to be kind to myself each day. It is not always easy, but I try. Life does go on."[58]

"Grief Ruled Me"

Like Meinecke, Kathy Whelan also lost a baby boy to SIDS. Michael, whom his parents called Mikey, died in 1990 when he was four months old. Whalen still grieves for him today. She vividly recalls the suffering she went through after his death. "In the early days, grief ruled me," she says. "I lived minute by minute. I willed myself to get out of bed, to take a shower, to breathe another breath. The clock didn't move without me thinking about my son. Missing his warm breath on my face. I lost my dreams when he died, and I didn't have the courage to dream again. I lived an unthinkably frightening nightmare."[59] About three weeks after Mikey died, Whelan went to her aerobics class. She had continued to go throughout her pregnancy, and the other women knew her baby was a boy. But because she did not socialize with them outside of class, no one there knew about Mikey's death. She could not bear the thought of telling them about it and watching their shocked reactions. She not only feared what they might say to her, she was also afraid of how she would feel as she told them. She was not able to face that, so she decided to keep silent. As the class progressed, however, she became overwhelmed with sadness and had to leave. She sat in her car, looking at the empty car seat that had once held her son, and she sobbed as she mourned his death. After that she intentionally avoided situations where she might see acquaintances who did not know her baby had died, and she continued to do so for several years.

Tamblin also recalls how difficult it was to face people after her son's death because in trying to comfort her, they made her feel worse. "I am convinced that most people do not have a clue what to say to a grieving parent," she says. Tamblin explains:

> This is really not brain surgery—all they have to say is, "I'm sorry" or "I loved him too" or "I'm here for you" but do they stop there? Oh no. They always have to offer words of advice and even though they may not realize the effect it has on grieving parents, they come off sounding totally callous. When people said to me, "He's in a better place," or "In time you won't feel so sad anymore," I seriously wanted to scream at them. They hadn't lost a child. They hadn't lived through the hell that Ed and I did. They had no idea what we were going through, so how could they know what it was like? How did they know how long we would need to heal? But the worst, the very worst, was the people who actually had the nerve to say, "Well, at least you still have Jeremy," or "You're still young, you'll have more children." I seriously wanted to hit them in the mouth.[60]

Ingrid Doyle, a woman from Ireland, lost her seven-month-old daughter to SIDS, and she, too, suffered because of people's reactions to the news of her baby's death. But in her case, it was because people avoided her. "Lots of people came to Hannah's funeral," she says. "There was an outpouring of grief. However, afterwards people found it hard to talk to us. Some would cross the street to avoid us. I know they felt uncomfortable, but all we wanted them to do was ask how we were and if we needed to talk, we would have let them know."[61]

Parents of SIDS victims sometimes avoid telling others about the death of their baby because even words of comfort can make them feel worse about the loss.

A Mother's Sadness

When parents lose a baby to SIDS, it is devastating for them. They all handle their grief in different ways. Often they reach out to others, as was the case with Jennifer Hernandez of Vallejo, California, who posted the following about her son's death on the Silent Grief *Web site:*

Well I am really not good at things like this, but I am hoping this will make me feel better before I lose it.... I lost my son William on March 8, 2002. He was only 3 months and 18 days old.... I can't even find the words to express the hurt and pain I feel about William's death. It had been just me and William from day one.... He was my sunshine. Just waking up to him every morning and seeing his smile made my day. Just having him in my life made me happy. I will never understand why? I tell myself every day he is in a much better place.... How am I [supposed] to go on and move forward when I feel like I just want to stay in bed with the blankets over my head? I don't go anywhere and I don't want to be around anyone. Even going to the cemetery to visit his grave is a task for me anymore, when I used to look forward to going. I know someone feels the same way I do. I am just rambling on and on. I guess I just need some support from others who know and feel my pain. Help?

Jennifer Hernandez, "My William," Silent Grief, December 13, 2002. www.silent grief.com/share/index.cgi?view_records=1&Category=SIDS+Loss&ID=580.

Plagued by Guilt

In addition to the grief people feel after losing a baby to SIDS, many suffer from extreme feelings of guilt. They begin to question everything they did, thinking that they were somehow responsible for their child's death. After Michael Bissonnette's son died from SIDS on Thanksgiving Day in 2005, he blamed himself for the baby's death. "I blamed myself a lot," he says, "because I was the one to lay him down. I was the one to feed him. Did I burp him enough? Should I have kept him up? I think 'should ofs' haunted me for a while afterward. Family and

Parents who lose a baby to SIDS sometimes wrestle with feelings of extreme guilt.

friends helped comfort me when I made those comments and could say, 'there's nothing you could have done.'"[62]

The National SIDS Resource Center says that Bissonnette's reaction is common among people who have lost children to SIDS. "SIDS parents also are very often plagued by 'if only's' that they are never able to resolve," the organization writes. "They mentally replay such thoughts as: 'If only I hadn't put the child down for a nap when I did.' 'If only I had checked on the baby sooner.' 'If only I had not returned to work so soon.' 'If only I had taken the baby to the doctor with that slight cold.'"[63] For these parents, it is little consolation that SIDS was diagnosed because it leaves so many questions unanswered. It is impossible for them to understand what caused their child's death because by its very definition, SIDS means there *was* no cause. Another problem is that many people do not know very much about SIDS or even know what it is. When SIDS unexpectedly claims the life of a baby, family members, friends, coworkers, and neighbors may be suspicious of the parents. This is especially true because SIDS strikes seemingly healthy babies with no warning. Being suspected of harming their child compounds the grief that parents are already suffering.

Tara Ahrens knows what it is like to feel the heart-wrenching grief and guilt after losing a child because her own baby boy died of SIDS. She writes: "People who have lost a child have endured the most awful and life-altering devastation a human can experience. Parents of SIDS babies, in particular, will suffer a life of grief, guilt, self-blaming and self-loathing, and they will never be the same. We will never feel that subsequent babies are 'safe,' 'healthy,' or 'just sleeping.'"[64] Ahrens becomes angry whenever she reads articles that attempt to explain why SIDS infants die, as though the deaths could have been prevented. She references one particular article that pinpointed things parents had done "wrong" that "caused" their babies to die, including smoking. Even though smoking is known as a risk factor, no one knows whether babies who die from SIDS after being exposed to smoke would have lived if they had not been exposed. "My son died for no reason," she says, "meaning, he was never exposed to smoke, was sleeping on his back in a climate-controlled car, was full-term and average birth weight. I took prenatal vitamins, got regular exercise while pregnant with him. I studied SIDS and was very informed and well prepared on how to 'prevent' it when he was born. I would love to know what anyone would tell me I did to cause my son to die."[65] Ahrens adds that the last thing grieving parents need is to read articles that list things they could have done and should have done in order to have kept their babies alive.

Placing Blame

Yet even the knowledge that they could not have prevented SIDS does little to console people whose babies have died from it. They are left feeling shocked and bewildered, wondering why their child had to die. Sometimes parents blame each other. According to pathologist Henry Krous, the impact on a couple of losing a baby is often devastating, and divorce is

The stress of losing a child to SIDS can sometimes cause parents to blame each other.

common in the aftermath of the death. Parents may also blame doctors who had pronounced that the baby was healthy right up until the time of death, or emergency medical personnel who could not save their baby. If the baby died while in day care, some parents blame the caregivers, erroneously believing that if they themselves had been there, their child would still be alive.

It is not uncommon for people who are suffering from horrible grief to blame God. They find themselves questioning God, wondering how he could be so cruel as to take their child. After Edge lost her daughter Kaitlyn to SIDS, she directed her anger toward God, as she explains: "It was so unfair and to this day I still feel like it is unfair. I used to look up at the sky and scream to God why? Why did he take my healthy, happy, and well-cared for baby, why? When there are so many abused and mistreated babies in the world. It was like nobody could answer that question. To this day I still ask WHY? I just want to know what I ever did to be so severely punished."[66]

Even people who have a strong spiritual faith often question why God would take their child. Todd and Angie Smith lost their baby nephew Luke to SIDS in May 2008. That would have been painful enough, but their own daughter, Audrey, had died of medical complications just seven weeks before. The Smiths, who were still grieving over the loss of their baby girl, were devastated over Luke's sudden, unexpected death. At the funeral home, Angie stood and looked down at him and could hear crying throughout the viewing room. She explains:

> Often times the guttural, aching sounds gave way to hushed prayer, and I realized that this is the mark of the believer in this horrifying moment. "Lord, I am empty, I am angry. I want it to be different. You could bring him back right this second if you so chose . . . but, it feels like for reasons we do not understand, you have chosen this instead . . . and so, we come humbly, barefoot, with our heads bowed, and we just ask for you to help us survive this grief." If we didn't need Him so much, we would all be tempted to turn our backs, I'm sure.[67]

"Life Is Insistent"

After a baby dies of SIDS, parents experience a wide range of emotions. They feel excruciating grief, as well as guilt, fear, and anger, and they wonder if life will ever be the same. They may blame each other, themselves, caregivers, or God. But as time passes, healing begins, and their pain diminishes a little more each day. Although they will never forget the child that they lost, they can and do eventually return to living again. Whelan shares her thoughts:

> How long must you grieve after your baby, the centre of your universe dies? I expect that I'll grieve for a lifetime. . . . But now I know what grief feels like and I'm not so scared about recovering from a particularly painful day. I'm not losing my sanity, I'm just grieving. What helps move your grief along is life. Life is insistent. There are other children to raise. Lunches to pack. Meetings to attend. And if I feel sad about Mikey, I don't fret. I cry because I loved him. I miss him. And there is nothing wrong with that.[68]

SIDS in the Future

Sudden infant death syndrome has often been called one of the most tragic medical mysteries. The idea that thousands of babies die for no apparent reason is unthinkable, yet it continues to happen year after year. By educating parents about known risk factors, researchers and health-care professionals are trying to reduce the prevalence of SIDS. Yet they are the first to admit that avoiding these risk factors is no guarantee against SIDS. Even infants who are exposed to no risk factors whatsoever still die of SIDS, while many others who are at higher risk do not. That is one reason why SIDS is so baffling, and it is also why scientists are fiercely committed to studying it. Their goal is to find the cause, or causes, of SIDS in an effort to put an end to this terrible killer of babies.

Experiments with Tadpoles

To support SIDS research, the National Institutes of Health (NIH) allocates nearly $80 million per year for research funding. Millions more are allocated for research by private SIDS foundations. One project that received a $1 million grant from the NIH is being conducted at the University of Alaska at Fairbanks (UAF). The research involves rather unusual laboratory creatures: tadpoles. Assistant professor Barbara Taylor explains why: "The tadpoles are a model we can use in experiments that would be difficult in rats or mice and impossible in humans. The brain stem, which sets the rhythm of breathing, is remarkably similar in tadpoles and humans. What we learn from our experiments on tadpoles may help us explain and prevent SIDS."[69] One reason why the UAF researchers are aggressively pursuing SIDS studies is that the prevalence of SIDS in Alaska is twice the national average. Among Alaskan Natives it is nearly four times higher than the national average. The focus of Taylor's research is to examine the effects smoking and alcohol have on babies who are still in the womb.

Scientists are studying tadpoles as part of their research on the causes of SIDS.

Using a microscope, researchers surgically remove a tadpole's tiny brain stem, which they are able to keep alive and "breathing" for up to three days. They add either alcohol or nicotine to the aquarium water to simulate prenatal exposure to these substances in order to determine how such exposure influences the brain stem's control of breathing. Taylor says they have found that exposure to alcohol and nicotine impairs the tadpoles' breathing responses to high carbon dioxide (hypercapnic response) and low oxygen (hypoxia response). "Such impaired responses, when they occur in human infants, are a factor in SIDS deaths," she says. Taylor continues:

> Babies born to mothers who smoke or drink during pregnancy have a higher risk of SIDS. The impairment of hypercapnic and hypoxic responses varies with the timing (when in development) and duration (how long it lasts) of exposure. Tadpoles can recover from the nicotine-induced impairment of their hypercapnic response if they are allowed a period of development when they are nicotine-free. We are currently determining if this recovery results from the regenerative capacity of amphibians or if mammals would be capable of such recovery. We have learned, however, that tadpoles cannot recover, with respect to breathing responses, from developmental exposure to alcohol.[70]

"SIDS Is Not a Mystery"

As with Taylor's research, laboratory animals are used in a number of SIDS studies, while others utilize the organs of humans who have died. The results of an infant brain study were announced in 2006 by researchers at the Children's Hospital in Boston and Harvard Medical School. The team examined the brains of thirty-one infants who had died of SIDS and compared them with the brains of ten infants who had died of other causes. Their focus was on an area of the brain known as the medulla oblongata, which is the lowest part of the brain stem. The medulla contains nerve cells that make and use serotonin, a chemical that transmits messages between nerve cells. Sero-

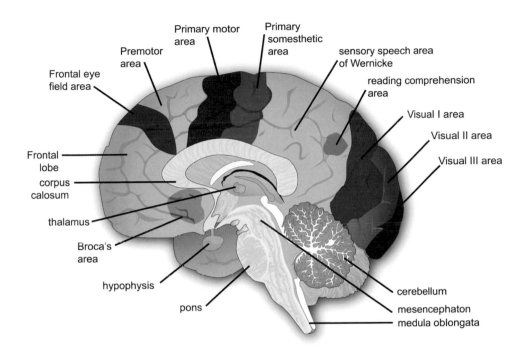

Researchers are focusing on the medulla oblongata (bottom, center) of the brain in their SIDS investigation.

tonin is known to help regulate sleep, appetite, and moods, as well as inhibit pain. It is also believed to help control breathing, blood pressure, sensitivity to carbon dioxide, and body temperature. The brains of the SIDS babies showed abnormalities in their serotonin systems. According to SIDS researcher Hannah Kinney, who coauthored the study, the team's findings indicate that SIDS is not as mysterious as researchers have long believed. Instead, they say that it is a biological problem. She explains: "SIDS is not a mystery. It's not something that parents did. SIDS is a disease. It's a scientific problem, and it can be tackled with scientific methods."[71] Kinney's team found that such brain defects occurred more often in male infants than in female infants. This could possibly unlock the secret of why baby boys die of SIDS much more often than baby girls.

The researchers also discovered that 65 percent of the SIDS victims had been sleeping on their stomachs. Kinney says that the brain defects that they observed could potentially reveal why stomach-sleeping babies die more often from SIDS than babies who sleep on their backs. She explains: "We feel that this kind of biological data gives an explanation to the 'Back to Sleep' messages, which might seem a little crazy at first blush. Why would putting a baby on its back save a life?" The reason, according to Kinney and the research team, is that SIDS babies may lack the reflex action that causes them to wake up and shift positions in order to get better air. "A normal baby would sense the low oxygen and turn its head and wake up,"[72] she says. If babies lack the ability to turn their heads to get better air, they continue to breathe in toxic carbon dioxide. Kinney adds that these sorts of abnormalities likely develop long before birth, while the infant is still in the mother's womb and the brain stem is developing. If that proves to be true, the research discoveries could eventually lead to the development of a diagnostic test that identifies babies who are at risk of developing SIDS.

Could SIDS Be Caused by Bacteria?

Scientists in the United Kingdom are also aggressively pursuing SIDS research. One study was published in the May 2008 issue of the British medical journal *Lancet*. It was based on the old theory that bacterial infection could play a role in some cases of unexplained infant deaths. In 1934, for instance, pathologist Sidney Farber published a report in the *New England Journal of Medicine*, in which he suggested that streptococcus infections in infants could be the cause of sudden infant death. For the new research, scientists at Great Ormond Street Hospital for Children in London analyzed the autopsies of nearly 500 infants who had died suddenly and unexpectedly between 1996 and 2005. The team organized the cases into three groups: autopsies that revealed no obvious cause of death; those that revealed a likely cause of bacterial infection; and those that revealed evidence of another cause that was not related to bacteria. High levels of *Staphylococcus aureus* (staph) and *E. coli* bacteria were found in 181 of the babies whose death could not be explained. These bacteria are commonly carried by

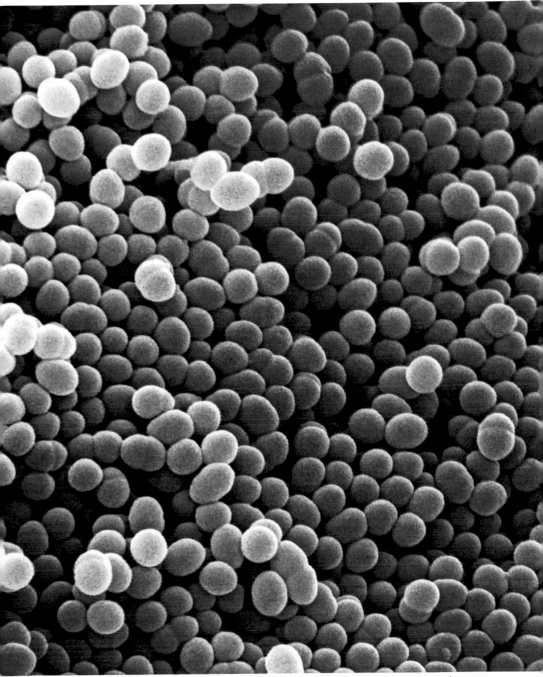

Researchers are studying if *staphylococcus aureus* bacteria may be linked to SIDS.

humans, generally in the nose and on the skin, and do not usually cause any harm. But in this study most of the bacteria were detected in the infants' lungs and spleens. This indicates that they played some sort of role in infection, which could have contributed to SIDS. The researchers say that this discovery could potentially help explain why SIDS deaths happen so quickly, with the transition from seemingly good health to death often occurring within as little as an hour. SIDS researcher James A. Morris explains: "The only way to imagine that this could occur is by the release of bacterial toxins into the bloodstream."[73] The research project expanded on Morris's 1999 study that showed heavier growths of bacteria in nasal samples taken from babies who slept on their stomachs compared with those who slept on their backs. The new findings reinforce the researchers' belief that bacterial infection might play a role in the development of SIDS in some babies. Morris explains: "If bacterial toxins are responsible for SIDS, this would explain why [back sleeping] improves survival. . . . The next step is not just to look for the bacteria in these babies, but to look for the toxins that the bacteria are producing. That is where this new science comes in."[74]

According to Cheryl Cipriani, a pediatric specialist from Texas, Morris's research does not necessarily prove that SIDS and dangerous bacteria are connected. She adds, however, that it could be an important component in the search for what causes SIDS. "This is another building block in our knowledge about these kinds of deaths," she says, "but association doesn't mean cause. But it's a large enough group of babies where you think the findings need to be paid attention to."[75]

"The Most Disastrous Thing That Can Happen"

Daniel Rubens is also searching for what causes SIDS. He is not a researcher nor even a SIDS specialist, but this is a priority for him, and he has developed an interesting theory. Rubens is an anesthesiologist at Seattle Children's Hospital and Regional Medical Center. His work involves putting babies to sleep and then monitoring their breathing while they undergo surgery. Over the years he has watched the babies of friends and acquaintances die from SIDS, and it frustrates him to see that a scientific understanding of SIDS is still lacking. "I'm a parent myself, I work with babies," he says. "SIDS is the most disastrous thing that can happen. [W]hen it comes to understanding why SIDS happens, I don't think we've moved very much at all."[76]

Several years ago Rubens began to wonder whether SIDS might be connected to the workings of the inner ear. He followed his intuition and decided to pursue the theory, as he explains: "I had the idea that we've missed something in medicine about the way the body controls breathing and that the missing piece might be in the specialized nerve tissue found in the inner ear."[77] Rubens decided to embark on his own study, and he turned to Susan Norton, an audiologist who has done extensive research on newborn hearing. Between 1993 and 2000 Norton led a national study to compare the effectiveness of various newborn hearing tests. Rubens and his colleagues analyzed an archive of the hearing tests. By comparing the test results of babies who had died of SIDS with other babies who survived, Rubens found that all of the SIDS babies had hearing deficiencies in the right ear. He believes that babies who die from SIDS suffer some sort of injury during birth. For instance, high levels of pressure and the mother's extended labor can disrupt blood flow, causing blood to course through the baby. This, says Rubens, can damage tiny, delicate hairs in the inner ear that are important for transmitting information to the brain about breathing and carbon dioxide levels in the blood. If these hairs are damaged, they are prevented from warning the brain about carbon dioxide levels so breathing can be adjusted. An infant who has this sort of dysfunction is at greater risk during sleep because breathing is slower and shallower than normal. Rubens says that SIDS babies suffocate because they are not getting enough oxygen.

Rubens's research findings have proved to be highly controversial. He has been challenged, and even scorned, by some other health-care professionals and researchers. Even some of his own colleagues questioned the validity of his study, as he

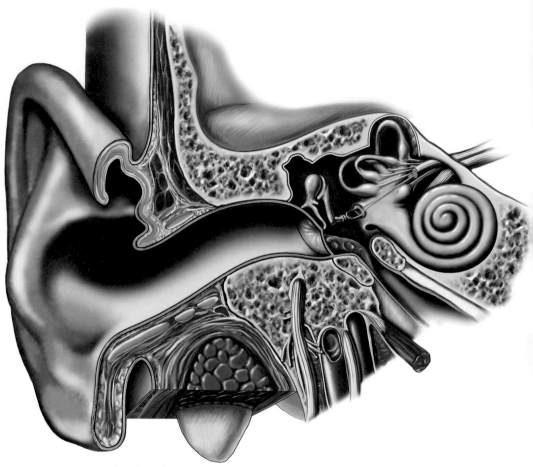

One researcher has theorized that damage to the inner ear can cause SIDS.

explains: "My impression was that they thought I was nuts."[78] Others, however, are curious about it and say that Rubens's discovery should be pursued in larger studies. If his theory is correct, a simple, standard hearing test could possibly detect SIDS in newborns.

The Genetic Link

While Rubens continues to examine the possible connection between inner ear injury and SIDS deaths, others are focusing on the role of genetics. Researchers at the Mayo Clinic have been studying the link between genes and SIDS for many years. In 2001 a team led by cardiologist Michael J. Ackerman announced that a cardiac gene known as SCN5A was clearly linked to SIDS. In 2005 researchers discovered that genes associated with a potentially fatal heart disorder known as long QT syndrome were present in 5 to 10 percent of SIDS cases. Long QT syndrome, which is a subtle electrical disturbance in the heart, is a medical condition that causes sudden, extremely rapid heart rates and can lead to potentially fatal heart rhythms known as arrhythmias. In May 2006 the Mayo Clinic researchers added two more cardiac genes to its list of potential links to SIDS. They say that the presence of these defective heart genes may cause as many as 15 percent of SIDS cases.

This photo shows amniotic fluid cells in a prenatal test for genetic mutations. Some scientists suggest that prenatal testing for defective genes can help identify babies that are at risk for SIDS.

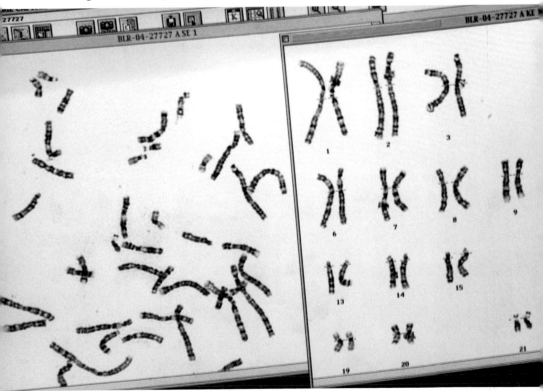

Researchers from Vanderbilt University are also pursuing genetic studies, and in January 2007 they published their most recent findings. The team found that nearly 10 percent of SIDS victims had mutations or variations in several different genes that are associated with arrhythmias. According to genomics researcher Alfred L. George Jr., senior author of one of the studies, the findings also suggest that testing infants could help identify whether they carry these defective genes. He explains: "We are not recommending that a population-wide genetic screening be done, but there may be simpler, cost-effective measures that should be investigated further, perhaps performing ECG (electrocardiogram) screening of infants, although this idea is controversial."[79] George adds that inherited arrhythmias are manageable conditions that can be treated with medications or implantable devices. Thus, if such defects were to be found in infants, they could receive treatment and possibly avoid being victims of SIDS.

George and the other researchers continue to analyze other genes that are linked to arrhythmias. They are also planning studies that will determine if the parents of SIDS victims carry the same mutations. "This is critical because knowing how often mutations are transmitted from parents rather than occur spontaneously, will help establish the risk to siblings of SIDS victims," he says. His hope is that eventually scientists will be able to identify all the causes of SIDS, including genetic factors as well as environmental and developmental factors. He explains: "Many years from now, 'SIDS' may not be a term we use anymore because we will understand all causes of sudden infant death. But right now, SIDS is a bona fide disease category, and we should strive to understand it fully."[80]

A Federal Mandate

Because SIDS is still so poorly understood, scientific research is essential in order to find what causes it and how it can be prevented. Another important step is for SIDS diagnoses to be more accurate than they are today. The Scripps Howard studies have revealed how inconsistent coroners and other health-care professionals are in diagnosing SIDS. Theresa Covington,

SIDS Decline or Sloppy Reporting?

A Scripps Howard study published in October 2007 reported that there was "enormous variation in how the deaths of infants are investigated and classified. The SIDS rate, according to the data, is 12 times higher in Mississippi than in New York. Most experts agree that the big differences are caused by how the deaths are classified, not by how the babies died." One finding of the study was that in 2003, the Mississippi legislature passed a law ordering state coroners to conduct death scene investigations for all sudden infant deaths. In 2002, before the new law was passed, the number of reported cases of SIDS was fifty-four; afterward, it jumped to ninety-four cases.

Thomas Hargrove and Lee Bowman, "Saving Babies: Exposing Sudden Infant Death in America," Scripps Howard News Service, October 8, 2007. http://scripps news.s10113.gridserver.com.

The lack of nationwide standards on how coroners determine when a death is caused by SIDS has resulted in inconsistent statistics on SIDS deaths.

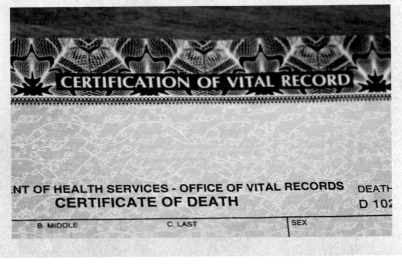

director of the University of Michigan's National Center for Child Death Review Policy and Practice, explains: "There's no rhyme or reason to what medical examiners are diagnosing as SIDS, suffocation, strangulation or undetermined. The variability is across the country and within the states."[81] The problem, as pointed out by the studies, is that the quality of infant death investigations, the level of training for coroners, and the amount of oversight and review vary widely across the country. The result is that many babies who are diagnosed as having died of SIDS actually died from other causes—and if those causes had been known, their deaths may have been prevented. James Kemp, who is a leading SIDS researcher at St. Louis University, says that the lack of a countrywide standard approach to investigating and classifying infant deaths hinders SIDS research and puts babies at risk.

In June 2008 then–U.S. senator Barack Obama proposed legislation that would improve the way America investigates and accounts for sudden infant deaths. If passed, the bill would provide funding for federal public health agencies, including the CDC, to set up national registries of sudden, unexpected infant deaths. Having access to such a vast database would help researchers better understand the causes and trends related to the deaths. Specifically, Obama's bill calls for the development of a surveillance and monitoring system that is based on thorough and complete death scene investigation data, clinical history, and autopsy findings. It also calls for a system of collecting standardized information about the environmental, medical, social, and genetic circumstances surrounding infant deaths. Another component is the establishment of a standardized classification system for defining subcategories of SIDS and SUID for surveillance and prevention research activities.

A number of SIDS groups have endorsed the proposed legislation, including the AAP's Task Force on SIDS, the American SIDS Alliance, and First Candle, among others. Marian Sokol, president of First Candle, explains her group's reaction: "First Candle applauds Sen. Obama for introducing this groundbreaking bill. Without consistency in defining, investigating and reporting these tragic deaths, families are left searching

In 2008, as a U.S. senator, Barack Obama proposed legislation to improve investigations into sudden infant deaths.

for answers and there is no hope for a future where these deaths can be prevented."[82]

Looking Toward Tomorrow

No one doubts that sudden infant death syndrome is a tragic, mystifying baby killer. Scientists have identified many risk factors and have educated the public about them, but still, all babies are at risk for SIDS. Even with all the research that has been done, the cause of SIDS remains unknown, and it cannot be prevented. However, progress is being made. Brain studies, genetic studies, and other sophisticated research, along with improved diagnostic techniques, are bringing scientists closer to a better understanding of SIDS. Hopefully, in the same way that numerous childhood diseases and disorders have been conquered, SIDS will someday be conquered as well. Jessica Tamblin shares her thoughts:

> I'm always ecstatic when I hear on the news about all the SIDS research that's being done, and how scientists are looking so hard to find a cause and how it can be prevented. I will admit that was somewhat bittersweet for me, though. I am so very hopeful that they'll succeed so not one more parent has to lose a precious child. But no matter what they do, or when they do it, it's already too late for my baby. And that's the really, really hard part.[83]

Notes

Introduction: "In One Moment My Life Shattered"

1. Cathy Meinecke, "From My Perspective," Iowa SIDS Foundation, Fall 2006. www.iowasids.org/Resources/Fall%20200 6%20Newsletter.pdf.
2. Bob Cringely, "Chase Cringely: Finding Meaning in a Lost Life," *I Cringely, The Pulpit*, April 25, 2002. www.pbs.org/cringely/ pulpit/ 2002/pulpit_20020425_000431.html.
3. Quoted in Thomas Hargrove and Lee Bowman, "SIDS Explanation Often Hollow, Yet Comforting," *Memphis Commercial Appeal*, October 7, 2007. www.commercialappeal. com/news/2007/Oct/07/sids-explanation-often-hollow-yet-comforting.
4. Rachal Tallent, "Jaiden Arien Glen Tallent: His Story," SIDS Families, June 12, 2007. www.sidsfamilies.com/index.php?scc=nursery3&id=2710&Jaiden_Arien_Glen_Tallent.

Chapter One: What Is SIDS?

5. D.L. Russell-Jones, "Sudden Infant Death in History and Literature," *Archives of Disease in Childhood*, 1985, p. 278.
6. Quoted in Russell-Jones, "Sudden Infant Death in History and Literature," p. 280.
7. J. Bruce Beckwith, "Defining the Sudden Infant Death Syndrome," *Archives of Pediatric & Adolescent Medicine*, March 2003, p. 287.
8. Beckwith, "Defining the Sudden Infant Death Syndrome," p. 287.
9. Quoted in Centers for Disease Control and Prevention, "Sudden Infant Death Syndrome—United States, 1980–1988," *Morbidity and Mortality Weekly Report*, July 17, 1992. www. cdc.gov/mmwR/preview/mmwrhtml/00017250.htm.

10. Angi Suby, "Stephen Paul: His Story," SIDS Families, 2007. www.sidsfamilies.com/index.php?sec=nursery3&id=2784& Stephen_Paul_#story.

11. Melissa Eason, "My Boy Cooper," SIDS Families, October 2006. www.sidsfamilies.com/index.php?sec=nursery3&id= 2345&Cooper_Joshua_Eason.

12. American SIDS Institute, "Reducing the Risk of SIDS." www.sids.org/nprevent.htm.

13. Quoted in Thomas Hargrove and Lee Bowman, "Saving Babies: Exposing Sudden Infant Death in America," Scripps Howard News Service, October 8, 2007. www.shns.com/ shns/g_index2.cfm?action=detail&pk=SIDS-SHORT-10-08-07.

14. Quoted in Hargrove and Bowman, "Saving Babies."

15. Kimberly de Montbrun, "How Bed Sharing Saved My Baby," GentleParents.com, Spring 2001. www.gentleparents.com/ articledemontbrun1.html.

16. De Montbrun, "How Bed Sharing Saved My Baby."

17. De Montbrun, "How Bed Sharing Saved My Baby."

18. Jessica Jackson, "Ethan William Lee Jackson: His Story," SIDS Families, 2007. www.sidsfamilies.com/index.php?sec =nursery3&id=2897&Ethan_William_Lee_Jackson.

Chapter Two: What Causes SIDS?

19. Jessica Tamblin, interview with author, June 2, 2008.

20. Tamblin, interview with author.

21. Tamblin, interview with author.

22. Linda Folden Palmer, "Cosleeping & SIDS," BabyReference.com, October 2005. www.babyreference.com/Cosleep ing&SIDS 2005 Review of the Studies.htm.

23. Palmer, "Cosleeping & SIDS."

24. Quoted in Palmer, "Cosleeping & SIDS."

25. James J. McKenna and Thomas McDade, "Why Babies Should Never Sleep Alone: A Review of the Co-sleeping Controversy in Relation to SIDS, Bedsharing and Breastfeeding," *Paediatric Respiratory Reviews*, 2005, p. 47.

26. De Montbrun, "How Bed Sharing Saved My Baby."

27. Betty McEntire, "Featured Question and Answer," American SIDS Institute. http://sids.org/nfeaturedques.htm.

28. American Academy of Pediatrics Task Force on Sudden Infant Death Syndrome, "The Changing Concept of Sudden Infant Death Syndrome: Diagnostic Coding Shifts, Controversies Regarding the Sleeping Environment, and New Variables to Consider in Reducing Risk," *Pediatrics*, November 2005. http://aappolicy.aappublications.org/cgi/content/full/pediatrics;116/5/1245.
29. Quoted in Brian Braiker, "A Quiet Revolt Against the Rules on SIDS," *New York Times*, October 18, 2005. www.nytimes.com/2005/10/18/health/18slee.html.
30. Quoted in Dan Ullrich, "Sudden Infant Deaths Decline; but Causes Remain a Mystery," Medical College of Wisconsin *HealthLink*, May 29, 2007. http://healthlink.mcw.edu/article/1031002757.html.
31. Quoted in Ted Koren, "Crib Death or Vaccine Death?" *Chiropractic Journal*, May 1994. www.worldchiropracticalliance.org/tcj/1994/may/may1994d.htm.
32. Quoted in JoNel Aleccia, "Shot in the Dark," *Spokesman Review*, December 23, 2007. www.spokesmanreview.com/breaking/story.asp?ID=12892.
33. Quoted in Aleccia, "Shot in the Dark."
34. Quoted in Aleccia, "Shot in the Dark."
35. Quoted in Braiker, "A Quiet Revolt Against the Rules on SIDS."

Chapter Three: The SIDS Diagnosis

36. American Academy of Pediatrics, "Distinguishing Sudden Infant Death Syndrome from Child Abuse Fatalities," *Pediatrics*, February 2001, p. 438.
37. Ernest H. Weyand, "Sudden, Unexplained Infant Death Investigations," *FBI Law Enforcement Bulletin*, March 2004. www.fbi.gov/publications/leb/2004/mar2004/march2004.htm.
38. American Academy of Pediatrics, "Distinguishing Sudden Infant Death Syndrome from Child Abuse Fatalities," p. 438.
39. Darlene Buth, "How NOT to Treat a SIDS Survivor," SIDS Network, Spring 1997. http://sids-network.org/fp/buth.htm.
40. Buth, "How NOT to Treat a SIDS Survivor."
41. Buth, "How NOT to Treat a SIDS Survivor."

42. Buth, "How NOT to Treat a SIDS Survivor."

43. Quoted in Patrick Bellamy, "Her Father's Daughter—the Kathleen Folbigg Story," Tru TV Crime Library, 2003. www. trutv.com/library/crime/notorious_murders/women/folbigg /index.html.

44. Quoted in Bellamy, "Her Father's Daughter."

45. Quoted in Bellamy, "Her Father's Daughter."

46. Quoted in Bellamy, "Her Father's Daughter."

47. Quoted in Thomas Hargrove and Lee Bowman, "Scripps Study on SIDS Focuses on Accidental Suffocation," *Knoxville (TN) News Sentinel*, December 22, 2007. www. knoxnews.com/news/2007/dec/22/scripps-study-sids-focuses-accidental-suffocation.

48. Quoted in Hargrove and Bowman, "Scripps Study on SIDS."

49. Kimberly Edge, "My Story and My Gratitude," Scripps News, *Saving Babies*, October 28, 2007. http://scrippsnews.s101 13.gridserver.com/node/34.

50. Kimberly Edge, "Important Question," comment to Lee Bowman, "The Trail of an Infant's Death," Scripps News, *Saving Babies*, October 28, 2007. http://scrippsnews.s101 13.gridserver.com/node/11.

Chapter Four: Surviving the Aftermath of SIDS

51. Eason, "My Boy Cooper."

52. Tamblin, interview with author.

53. Tamblin, interview with author.

54. Meinecke, "From My Perspective."

55. Meinecke, "From My Perspective."

56. Meinecke, "From My Perspective."

57. Meinecke, "From My Perspective."

58. Meinecke, "From My Perspective."

59. Kathy Whelan, "The First Year of Grief," *Baby's Breath*, March 2003. www.sidscanada.org/news/Babys_Breath_newsletter_March_2003.pdf.

60. Tamblin, interview with author.

61. Quoted in Jacqueline Kavanagh, "How We Learned to Live Again After Losing Hannah," *Independent* (Ireland), May 5,

2008. www.independent.ie/lifestyle/parenting/how-we-learned-to-live-again-after-losing-hannah-1367122.html.

62. Quoted in Alexi Howk, "Finding Help After SIDS Death of Son Was Difficult, Palm Bay Couple Say," *TC Palm*, October 7, 2007. www.tcpalm.com/news/2007/oct/07/finding-help-after-sids-death-son-was-difficult-pa.

63. National SIDS Resource Center, "The Death of a Child—the Grief of the Parents: A Lifetime Journey," September 1997. www.athealth.com/consumer/disorders/parentalgrief.html.

64. Tara Ahrens, "Parents Whose Babies Died from SIDS Deserve Support," Baby Mine Store, January 22, 2007. www.babyminestore.com/newsparentsbabiesdiedsids.html.

65. Ahrens, "Parents Whose Babies Died from SIDS Deserve Support."

66. Edge, "My Story and My Gratitude."

67. Angie Smith, "Sweet Baby Lukie," *Bring the Rain*, May 30, 2008. http://audreycaroline.blogspot.com/2008/05/sweet-baby-lukie.html.

68. Whelan, "The First Year of Grief."

Chapter Five: SIDS in the Future

69. Quoted in Sonja Bickford, "Tadpoles Used in SIDS Research at UAF," *UAF Newsroom*, June 2006. www.uaf.edu/news/featured/06/sids/index.html.

70. Barbara Taylor, e-mail interview with author, June 27, 2008.

71. Quoted in Nancy Shute, "Solving the SIDS Mystery," *U.S. News & World Report*, November 5, 2006. http://health.usnews.com/usnews/health/articles/061105/13sids.htm.

72. Quoted in Nancy Shute, "Children's Health: The Deadly Secrets of Sudden Infant Death Syndrome," *U.S. News & World Report*, October 31, 2006. http://health.usnews.com/usnews/health/articles/061031/31health.sids.htm.

73. Quoted in Salynn Boyles, "Bacteria May Be Linked to SIDS," WebMD, May 29, 2008. http://children.webmd.com/news/20080529/bacteria-may-be-linked-to-sids.

74. Quoted in Boyles, "Bacteria May Be Linked to SIDS."

75. Quoted in Amanda Gardner, "Bacterial Infection May Boost SIDS Risk," *Washington Post*, May 30, 2008. www.washing

tonpost.com/wp-dyn/content/article/2008/05/29/AR20080
52903472.html.

76. Quoted in Andrea Pitzer, "Provocative New Theory on Sudden Infant Death," *USA Today*, September 30, 2007. www.usatoday.com/news/health/2007-09-30-SIDS-theory _N.htm.

77. Quoted in Children's Hospital and Regional Center, "Listening to a Hunch," *Connection*, Winter 2008. http://research.seattlechildrens.org/assets/docs/connection_rubens_article.pdf.

78. Quoted in Pitzer, "Provocative New Theory."

79. Quoted in *Medical News Today*, "Heart Rhythm Genes Possible Factor in SIDS," January 18, 2007. www.medicalnewstoday.com/articles/60902.php.

80. Quoted in *Medical News Today*, "Heart Rhythm Genes Possible Factor in SIDS."

81. Quoted in Hargrove and Bowman, "Saving Babies."

82. Quoted in Lee Bowman and Thomas Hargrove, "Obama Proposes Legislation to Better Track SIDS, Stillbirths," Barack Obama: U.S. Senator for Illinois, June 16, 2008.

83. Tamblin, interview with author.

Glossary

apnea: An absence of breathing.

apparent life-threatening event (ALTE) syndrome: A sudden, unexpected change in an infant's breathing that can cause change in skin color, apnea, or choking and gagging.

arrhythmia: A potentially fatal irregular heartbeat that, if discovered, can be treated with medicines or implants.

brain stem: A stalk of nerve cells and fibers that links the lowest part of the brain to the spinal cord.

infanticide: The intentional murder of an infant.

medulla oblongata: The lowest portion of the brain stem that regulates such functions as breathing and blood pressure.

serotonin: A brain chemical that transmits messages between nerve cells and is known to help regulate sleep, appetite, and moods, as well as inhibit pain.

Organizations to Contact

American SIDS Institute
509 Augusta Dr.
Marietta, GA 30067
phone: (770) 426-8746 or toll-free: (800) 232-7437
fax: (770) 426-1369
Web site: www.sids.org

Through research, clinical services, education, and family support, the American SIDS Institute seeks to prevent sudden infant death and promote infant health. The Web site offers general information about SIDS as well as research findings, statistics, and articles.

Canadian Foundation for the Study of Infant Deaths (CFSID)
60 James St., Ste. 403
St. Catharines, ON L2R 7E7
phone: (905) 688-8884 or toll-free: (800) 363-7437
fax: (905) 688-3300
e-mail: sidsinfo@sidscanada.org
Web site: www.sidscanada.org

The CFSID is dedicated to reducing infant mortality and the rate of sudden and unexpected infant deaths, as well as providing emotional support to those who have been affected by them. The Web site offers news releases, statistics, research findings, tips for parents, and a newsletter called *Baby's Breath*.

The Compassionate Friends
PO Box 3696
Oak Brook, IL 60522-3696
phone: (630) 990-0010 or toll-free: (877) 969-0010
fax: (630) 990-0246
Web site: www.compassionatefriends.org

The Compassionate Friends is a nonprofit self-help organization that assists families who have lost a child and provides information that helps others be supportive. The Web site offers a weekly Web-based radio news show titled *Healing the Grieving Heart*, a series of "Grief in the News" articles, brochures, and fact sheets.

First Candle
1314 Bedford Ave., Ste. 210
Baltimore, MD 21208
phone: (800) 221-7437
e-mail: info@firstcandle.org
Web site: www.sidsalliance.org

A product of the SIDS Alliance, First Candle's mission is to unite parents, caregivers, and researchers with government, business, and community service groups to advance infant health and survival. The Web site offers position statements, research studies, statistics on deaths from SIDS and other causes of infant mortality, and a newsletter called *Illuminations*.

Foundation for the Study of Infant Deaths (FSID)
Artillery House
11–19 Artillery Row
London, United Kingdom SW1P 1RT
phone: +44 (0)207 222-8001
fax: +44 (0)207 222-8002
e-mail: office@fsid.org.uk
Web site: www.sids.org.uk

The FSID seeks to prevent unexpected infant deaths and promote infant health by funding research, providing support to families who have lost babies unexpectedly, working with professionals to improve investigations after a baby dies, and distributing information related to infant health, baby care, and sudden infant deaths to health professionals and the public. The Web site offers news stories, press releases, research findings, and parents' stories.

National Sudden Infant Death Resource Center (NSIDRC)
2115 Wisconsin Ave. NW, Ste. 601
Washington, DC 20007-2292
phone: (202) 687-7466 or toll-free: (866) 866-7437
fax: (202) 784-9777
e-mail: info@sidscenter.org
Web site: www.sidscenter.org

The NSIDRC serves as a centralized source of information on sudden infant death and on promoting health for infants from the prenatal period through the first year of life and beyond. The Web site offers statistics, an "A to Z" topic section, research studies, and journal alerts.

Project IMPACT
Administrative Offices
112 E. Allegan, Ste. 500
Lansing, MI 48933
DC Regional Office
8280 Greensboro Dr., Ste. 300
McLean, VA 22102
phone: (800) 930-7437
fax: (517) 485-0163
Web site: www.sidsprojectimpact.com

Project IMPACT is a cooperative agreement between the federal Maternal and Child Health Bureau and the Association of SIDS and Infant Mortality Programs. The organization supports state and local infant death programs through information sharing, promoting policy and legislative changes, and fostering partnerships and communication. The Web site offers research, a "News and Events" section, and links to other resources.

Sudden Infant Death Syndrome (SIDS) Network
PO Box 520
Ledyard, CT 06339
e-mail: sidsnet1@sids-network.org
Web site: www.sids-network.org

The SIDS Network seeks to eliminate SIDS by supporting research projects, providing support for people who have experienced the trauma of a SIDS death, and raising public awareness of SIDS through education. A wealth of information can be found on its Web site, including articles, FAQs, research findings, and statistics.

For Further Reading

Books

Monica Cane, *A Journey to Healing: Life After SIDS.* San Leandro, CA: Jireh, 2004. This is a mother's story of the grief of losing her baby to SIDS and how she eventually healed and found peace.

Dawne J. Gurbutt, *Sudden Infant Death Syndrome: Learning from Stories About SIDS, Motherhood and Loss.* Abingdon, UK: Radcliffe, 2007. This book features real-life accounts of mothers who have lost babies to SIDS.

Wolfgang Rietig, *"Phenomenon": Sudden Infant Death Finally Understood.* Norderstedt, Germany: Books on Demand, 2007. This book explains what SIDS is, what the risk factors are, and steps parents can take to possibly avoid losing a child to it.

Periodicals

Martha Brant and Anna Kuchment, "The Little One Said 'Roll Over,'" *Newsweek*, May 29, 2006. An interesting article about the pros and cons of co-sleeping.

Claudia Kalb, "Big Binkie Brouhaha," *Newsweek*, October 31, 2005. An article about the theory that pacifiers may help protect babies against SIDS.

Tom Matthews, "Sudden Unexpected Infant Death: Infanticide or SIDS?" *Lancet*, January 1, 2005. Examines the small number of infant deaths that are due to child abuse rather than SIDS.

J. Rehmeyer, "Abated Breath," *Science News*, November 4, 2006. Discusses studies that show that the brain chemical serotonin may play a role in SIDS deaths.

Internet Sources

Brian Braiker, "A Quiet Revolt Against the Rules on SIDS," *New*

York Times, October 18, 2005. www.nytimes.com/2005/10/18/ health/18slee.html. Examines the various perspectives of having babies sleep on their stomachs versus their backs.

Thomas Hargrove and Lee Bowman, "Scripps Study on SIDS Focuses on Accidental Suffocation," *Knoxville (TN) News Sentinel,* December 22, 2007. www.knoxnews.com/news/ 2007/dec/22/scripps-study-sids-focuses-accidental-suffocation. Examines the inconsistencies of investigations after infants die, which can lead to incorrect diagnoses.

Lisa Hoffman, "When an Angel Dies," *Knoxville (TN) News Sentinel,* October 8, 2007. www.knoxnews.com/news/2007/Oct/ 08/when-angel-dies. The story of Aaron and Rachal Tallent whose son, Jaiden, died of SIDS at the age of three and a half weeks.

Jacqueline Kavanagh, "How We Learned to Live Again After Losing Hannah," *Independent (Ireland),* May 5, 2008. www.inde pendent.ic/lifestyle/parenting/how-we-learned-to-live-again- after-losing-hannah-1367122.html. The story of one family's struggle after losing a seven-month-old baby to SIDS.

Andrew Pitzer, "Provocative New Theory on Sudden Infant Death," *USA Today,* September 30, 2007. www.usatoday. com/news/health/2007-09-30-SIDS-theory_N.htm. Examines the theory of pediatric anesthesiologist Daniel Rubens that a birthing injury at the time of delivery could lead to SIDS.

Nancy Shute, "Solving the SIDS Mystery," *U.S. News & World Report,* November 4, 2006. http://health.usnews.com/us news/health/articles/061105/13sids.htm. Discusses the progress researchers have made in studying brain abnormalities in SIDS victims.

Web Sites

Centers for Disease Control and Prevention (CDC) (www. cdc.gov). Numerous articles about SIDS are accessible through this Web site and cover topics such as SIDS statistics, whether vaccinations play a role in SIDS, risk factors among minorities, and prevention guidelines.

How Stuff Works (www.howstuffworks.com). A number of informative articles about SIDS can be found on this Web site, including "The Causes of SIDS," "Overcoming Guilt About SIDS," and "Have Scientists Discovered What Causes SIDS?" among others.

Mayo Clinic: Sudden Infant Death Syndrome (www.mayo clinic.com/health/sudden-infant-death-syndrome/DS00145). This site contains extensive information about SIDS, including what it is, possible causes/risk factors, prevention, and coping skills.

National Institutes of Health (NIH) (www.nichd.nih.gov). The NIH site is an excellent resource for SIDS-related information such as risk factors, research findings, myths and facts, and details about the Back to Sleep campaign.

SIDS Families (www.sidsfamilies.com). Created by a woman in memory of the baby she lost to SIDS, this site offers hundreds of real-life stories about SIDS deaths, as well as SIDS statistics, a glossary of terms, risk factors, and various theories about what causes SIDS.

Index

A

Abramson, Harold, 12–13
Ackerman, Michael J., 79
African American infants, 18
Ahrens, Tara, 66–67
Alaska, 71
Alcohol, 71–72
American Academy of
  Pediatrics (AAP), 15, 27–28
Anger, 58, 68
Apnea, 21, 22
Apparent life-threatening event
  syndrome (ALTE), 20–23
Arizona, 48
Arrhythmias, 79–80
Asphyxiation, 52–55
Australia, 33
Autopsies, 42–45

B

Back sleeping, 31–34
Back to Sleep campaign, 33
Bacteria, 74–76
Beckwith, J. Bruce, 13–14
Bed sharing, 27–31
Bissonnette, Michael, 64, 66
Blame, 67–68
Botulism, 44
Boys, 18, 73
Brain research, 71–74
Brain stem, 71, 72–73
Buth, Darlene, 45–46, 48

C

Carbon dioxide, 32–33, 74
Cardiac genes, 79–80
Centers for Disease Control and
  Prevention (CDC), 18
Central nervous system,
  34, 36
Child abuse, 48, 52
Cigarette smoking, 34–37, *35*,
  66–67, 71–72
Cipriani, Cheryl, 76
Coroners, 20, *43*, 44–45
Co-sleeping, 27–31, *29*
Covington, Theresa, 80, 82
Crib death. *See* SIDS (Sudden
  Infant Death Syndrome)
Crib mattresses, 30
Cringely, Bob, 6, 8
Curgenven, Brendon, 28

D

De Montbrun, Kimberly, 22–23,
  31
Death certificates, *81*
Deaths. *See* Infant deaths
Diagnosis, 13–14, 40, 52–55,
  80–84
Diphtheria, tetanus, and
  pertussis (DTP) vaccine, 36
Divorce, 67–68
Doyle, Ingrid, 62
Dupuis, Meta, 45

E
E. coli, 74, 76
Eason, Cooper Joshua, 16–17
Eason, Melissa, 56
Edge, Kimberley, 54–55, 68
England, 33

F
Family beds, 27–31, *29*
Farber, Sidney, 74
Fear, 58, 61
Federal Bureau of Investigation
   (FBI), 10, 40
First Candle, 82
Folbigg, Craig, 51
Folbigg, Kathleen, 51–52

G
Garrow, Irene, 12–13
Gender, 18, 73
Genetics, 78–80
George, Alfred L., Jr., 80
Gershen, William H., 34
Girls, 18, 73
Grief, *24*, 56–64, *57*, *63*, 69
Guilt, 64–67, *65*

H
Hall, Karen, 23
Haynes, Tom, 54
Heart conditions, 79–80
Hepatitis, 10
Hernandez, Jennifer, 64
Hong Kong, 31

I
Idaho, 48, 51
Infant botulism, 44

Infant deaths
   classification of, 20,
      80–84
   by homicide, 48–52
   investigations of, 40–48,
      46–47, 52–54, 82–84
   number of, *17*, 18
   by race, *17*
   from SIDS, 6, 8, 10
   See also SIDS (Sudden Infant
      Death Syndrome)
Infanticides, 48–52
Infants
   age of, 14, 16–17
   characteristics of SIDS, 14
   gender of, 18, 73
   premature, *16*, 18
   sleeping with, 27–31, *29*
Infections, 74–76
Inner ear, 77–*78*
Institute for SIDS Research,
   27

J
Jackso, Jessica, 23
Japan, 31

K
Karlsson, Leif, 36
Kattwinkel, John, 18, 39
Kemp, James, 82
Kinney, Hannah, 73–74
Krous, Henry, 8, 67–68

L
Leukemia, 10
Long QT syndrome, 79
Lyon, Erica, 34

M

Mattresses, 30

Mayo Clinic, 27, 78–79

McEntire, Betty, 31

McKenna, James J., 30, 31

Medical history, 42

Medulla oblongata, 72–74, *73*

Meinecke, Cathy, 58, 60–61

Meningitis, 10

Minyard, Andrea, 52

Mississippi, 81

Morris, James A., 76

Mothers

  age of, *16*, 18

  smoking by, 34–36, *35*, 71–72

  See also Parents

Munchausen syndrome by

  proxy (MSP), 50

Murders, 48–52, *49*

N

National Institute of Child

  Health and Human

  Development, 14, 27, 33

National Institutes of Health

  (NIH), 70

National SIDS Resource Center,

  66

National Vaccine Information

  Center, 36

Native Alaskan infants, 18, 71

Native American infants, 18

Near-miss SIDS, 21–22

New Zealand, 33

Norton, Susan, 77

O

Obama, Barack, 82, *83*

Omaha, Nebraska, 54

Ophoven, Janice, 52

P

Pacifiers, *19*

Palmer, Linda Folden, 29–30

Parents

  aftermath of SIDS for, 56–69,

   57, 63, 67

  compassion for, 45

  devastation felt by, 6, 8–9,

   23–25, *24, 57, 63*

  grief of, 56–64, 69

  guilt felt by, 64–67, *65*

  murder by, 48–52

  placing blame by, 67–68

  support groups for, *59*, 60

  as target of investigation,

   45–48

Paup, Harriet, *50*

Pediarix, 38

Pneumonia, 10

Poole, April, 8

Pregnancy

  alcohol use during, 71–72

  smoking during, 34–36,

   71–72

Premature infants, *16*, 18

Prenatal care, 18

R

Race, *17*, 18

Reiki technique, 60, 61

Research, 12–13, 70–80

Resuscitation, *21*

Risk factors, 14–18, 26–39, 70

Rubens, Daniel, 76–78

Russell-Jones, D.L., 12

Ryan, Bernard, 51, 52

S
Scheibner, Viera, 36, 38
SCN5A, 79
Scripps Howard study, 80, 81
Secondhand smoke, 34–36
Serotonin, 72–73
Siculus, Diodorus, 10
SIDS (Sudden Infant Death Syndrome)
   aftermath of, 56–69, *57, 63, 67*
   causes, 26–39
   deaths from, 6, 8, 10
   definition of, 13–14
   diagnosis of, 13–14, 40, 52–55, 80–84
   genetic links, 78–80
   in history, 10, 12
   mystery of, 8, 9, 38–39
   pacifiers and, *19*
   prevalence of, 18, 20
   race and, *17*
   research on, 12–13, 70–80
   risk factors, 14–18, 26–39, 70
   statistics on, 6, 17, 18
   vs. suffocation, 52–55
Smith, Angie, 68
Smith, Todd, 68
Smoking, 34–37, *35*, 66–67, 71–72
Sokol, Marian, 82
Staphylococcus aureus, 74–76
Steffke, Angie, 20

Stomach sleeping, *12*, 31–34, 73–74, 76
Streptococcus infections, 74
Stuffed animals, *32*
Suby, Angi, 14, 33
Sudden unexplained infant death (SUID) investigations, 40–48, 52–54, 82–84
Suffocation, 12–13, 28, 52–55
Support groups, *59*, 60

T
Tadpole experiments, 70–72, *71*
Tallent, Aaron, 8–9
Tallent, Rachal, 8–9
Tamblin, Ed, 26–27
Tamblin, Jessica, 26–27, 56, 58, 62, 84
Taylor, Barbara, 70–72
Teenage mothers, 18
Toxic gases, 30, 32–33

V
Vaccinations, 36–38, *37*
Victorian-era theories, 28

W
Walker, Shelly, 38
Werne, Jacob, 12–13
Weyand, Ernst H., 42
Whelan, Kathy, 61–62, 69

Z
Zalman, Barry, 23

Picture Credits

About the Author

Peggy J. Parks holds a bachelor of science degree from Aquinas College in Grand Rapids, Michigan, where she graduated magna cum laude. She is a freelance author who has written more than seventy nonfiction educational books for children and young adults. Parks lives in Muskegon, Michigan, a town that she says inspires her writing because of its location on the shores of Lake Michigan.